NOT A
NOT Be
&C

Lance Strate

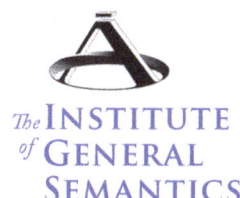

The INSTITUTE
of GENERAL
SEMANTICS

Copyright © 2024 by Lance Strate

All rights reserved. No part of this publication may be reproduced or transmitted in any form or by any means, electronic or mechanical, including photocopying, recording, or by any information storage and retrieval system, without permission in writing from the publisher.

Published by the Institute of General Semantics
401 Park Avenue South #873
New York, NY, 10016
www.generalsemantics.org

Interior Book Design by Scribe Freelance
www.scribefreelance.com

ISBN: 978-1-970164-27-5 (Print)
978-1-970164-28-2 (eBook)
Published in the United States of America

Library of Congress Cataloging-in-Publication Data

Names: Strate, Lance, author.
Title: Not a, not be, &c / Lance Strate.
Other titles: Not a, not be, and c
Description: New York, NY : Institute of General Semantics, 2024. | Includes bibliographical references and index. | Summary: "Not A, Not Be, &c is a collection of essays on general semantics and media ecology, based on the apporach that Alfred Korzybski referred to as a non-aristotelian. The lead essay begins with the concept of the non-aristotelian, also contextualizing and complementing general semantics by way of media ecology, and following Korzybski's lead by grounding it all in physics (and a bit of metaphysics). The second essay relates to the non-aristotelian principle of non-identity, as it reviews the differences between three different types of codes or symbol systems: language, images, and numbers/numerals. The third essay reviews the case against the verb "to be" in general semantics, and considers the broader context by way of linguistics and orality-literacy studies. The fourth essay consists of a reflection on the topic of imagination. The fifth essay combines concepts derived from general semantics and media ecology to provide suggestions for critical thinking. And the final essay reviews the extensional devices that Korzybski originally offered as general semantics correctives for ways in which language can mislead us about the nature of reality, offering a new extensional device, "the and," contextualized via orality-literacy studies"– Provided by publisher.
Identifiers: LCCN 2024022316 (print) | LCCN 2024022317 (ebook) | ISBN 9781970164275 (trade paperback) | ISBN 9781970164282 (epub)
Subjects: LCSH: General semantics. | Communication–Philosophy. | Mass media–Philosophy. | Mass media and language. | LCGFT: Essays.
Classification: LCC B820 .S76 2024 (print) | LCC B820 (ebook) | DDC 149/.94–dc23/eng/20240603
LC record available at https://lccn.loc.gov/2024022316
LC ebook record available at https://lccn.loc.gov/2024022317

Table of **Contents**

About the Author 1
Prolegomenon (Not Not An Introduction) 3
Acknowledgements 23

Index of Proper Names 25
Subject Index 29
References 35

Part 1   Not A **43**
Chapter 1 If Not A, Then E 45
Chapter 2 Word, Image, Number 69

Part 2   Not Be **89**
Chapter 3 It Is What It Isn't 91
Chapter 4 Figments of a Fragment, or Fragments of a
              Figment 137

Part 3   &c. **141**
Chapter 5 So You Want to Change the World? A
              Hitchhiker's Guide to Subversive Thinking 143
Chapter 6 The And 169

About the Author

Lance Strate received his BS degree at Cornell University where he majored in Communication Arts, went on to earn an MA degree from the Communication Arts and Sciences Department at Queens College of the City University of New York, and a PhD in the Media Ecology Program at New York University. He currently holds the position of Professor of Communication and Media Studies at Fordham University, where he has been teaching for 35 years (and counting). As a visiting scholar in 2015 he was selected as the Harron Family Chair in Communication at Villanova University, and was granted an honorary appointment as Chair Professor in the School of Journalism and Communication at Henan University in Kaifeng, China, in 2016.

Dr. Strate has served on the Board of Trustees of the Institute of General Semantics since 2013, and as IGS President since 2020, having previously served as Executive Director from 2008–2011. He also served as a member of the Board of Directors of the New York Society for General Semantics from 2009 to 2012, as President of the NYSGS from 2016 to 2021, and currently serves as NYSGS Secretary. One of the founders of the Media Ecology Association, he served as the MEA President for over a decade and remains a member of the MEA's Board of Directors. Professor Strate joined the Academic Board of Directors of the Global Listening Centre in 2016, served as Co-Chair of the Board from 2020 to 2023, and was appointed Senior Vice-President for Academic Affairs in 2023. Additionally, he served as President of Congregation Adas Emuno of Leonia, New Jersey for six years, from 2012 to 2018, and remains a member of their Board of Trustees.

Lance Strate has received a number of honors, including being selected to deliver the 66th Annual Alfred Korzybski Memorial Lecture in 2018 and receiving the Sanford I. Berman Award for Excellence in Teaching General Semantics in 2024 and the J. Talbot Winchell Award for Service in 2022 from the Institute of General Semantics, receiving the Outstanding Research Award from the Global Listening Centre in 2020, the Distinguished Research Fellow Award from the Eastern Communication Association in 2019, the Marshall McLuhan Award for Outstanding Book in 2018 and the Walter Ong Award for Career Achievement in Scholarship in 2013 from the Media Ecology Association, the Neil Postman Mentor Award in 2019 and the John F. Wilson Fellow Award for exceptional scholarship, leadership, and dedication to the field of communication in 1998 from the New York State Communication Association, and the Proclamation by Mayor Wellington E. Webb, in honor of his keynote address to the Rocky Mountain Communication Association, "that February 15, 2002 be known as Dr. Lance Strate Day in the City and County of Denver."

Lance Strate has authored and edited 18 books, including *First Letter of My Alphabet* (2023), *Concerning Communication: Epic Quests and Lyric Excursions Within the Human Lifeworld* (2022), *Diatribal Writes of Passage in a World of Wintertextuality* (2020), *Media Ecology: An Approach to Understanding the Human Condition* (2017), *Taking Up McLuhan's Cause: Perspectives on Media and Formal Causality* (2017), *Thunder at Darwin Station* (2015), *The Medium is the Muse: Channeling Marshall McLuhan* (2015), *Amazing Ourselves to Death: Neil Postman's Brave New World Revisited* (2014), *Korzybski and ...* (2012), *On the Binding Biases of Time and Other Essays on General Semantics and Media Ecology* (2011), and *Communication and Cyberspace: Social Interaction in an Electronic Environment* (1996, 2003). He has also served as editor of the *Speech Communication Annual*, the *General Semantics Bulletin*, and *Explorations in Media Ecology*, a journal he founded and edited for 9 years. Translations of his writing have appeared in French, Spanish, Italian, Portuguese, Hungarian, Hebrew, Mandarin, and Quenya.

Prolegomenon
(Not Not An **Introduction**)

Not A, Not Be, &c is not just another collection of essays on general semantics. Not that it is not exactly that, a collection of essays on general semantics specifically, and on what Neil Postman (1974) described as *general semantics writ large*, aka media ecology. Or to use the designation adopted by the Balvant Parekh Centre in Baroda, India, this is a collection of essays on *general semantics and other human sciences*. Alternately, this is a book devoted to essays in a *non-aristotelian* vein, which is what the first *not* in the title, *Not A*, refers to. *Non-aristotelian* is Alfred Korzybski's neologism, providing a name for a category of perspectives, and approaches that would include human sciences such as media ecology (Postman, 1970, 1974; Strate, 2017b), information theory (Shannon & Weaver, 1949), cybernetics (Bateson, 1972, 1979; Wiener, 1950, 1961), systems theory (Bateson, 2016, 2023; Bertalanffy, 1969), semiotics (Peirce, 1991), etc. And, of course, general semantics, as can be seen from the title of Korzybski's major work, originally published in 1933 and now in its sixth edition, *Science and Sanity: An Introduction to Non-Aristotelian Systems and General Semantics*, (Korzybski, 1933/2023).

And the second *not* in the title, *Not Be*, refers specifically to general semantics, and in particular to the critique regarding our use of the verb *to be* initiated by Korzybski and amplified by some of his followers. Following the two *nots* I have added *&c*, an abbreviation of *etc.*, itself an abbreviation of the Latin phrase, *et cetera*, literally meaning *and the rest*, which is to say, *and so forth* or *and other things*. *Etc.* is one of the three main extensional devices recommended by Korzybski, the intent being to counter the illusion that any statement can ever be complete or final and, as Mary P. Lahman (2018) incisively explains, to instill a sense of humility in all of us by reminding us of the limits of our knowledge, and our ability to communicate. In sum, the three parts of the title, *Not A, Not Be, &c*, all represent elements of the discipline of general semantics. And the title technically would be pronounced, "not A, not B, et cetera," but I had an added meaning in mind. It seems to me that at first glance, the title would be pronounced, "not A, not B, and C," bringing to mind the ABCs, and consequently serving as an allusion to the alphabet. The hidden reference would then be to the field of media ecology, as scholars such as Marshall McLuhan (1962, 1964), Walter Ong (1967, 1982), Jack Goody (1977), and Eric Havelock (1963, 1978, 1982, 1986) have discussed the pivotal role that alphabetic writing has played in the development of western culture, and the essential role that writing systems in general have played in the shift from tribal cultures to the more complex forms of social organization that traditionally have been associated with the term *civilization*. Korzybski (1950, 1933/2024) himself was aware of the enormous impact that writing had on our capacity for *time-binding*, the characteristic that he considered to be the defining trait of our species, our ability to preserve, accumulate, and evaluate knowledge over time, and thereby make progress.

I can therefore state with confidence that *Not A, Not Be, &c* is not not a book about media ecology. And *Not A, Not Be, &c* is most certainly not not a book about general semantics. And all of this negativity brings to mind one of my favorite linguistics jokes, about the famous scholar who was giving a keynote address at a major international linguistics conference. In his speech, he explained that while in some languages a double negative has a negative meaning—French for example, *n'est-ce pas?*, in other languages a double negative constitutes a positive—as in the pithy saying produced by Paul Watzlawick, Janet Beavin Bavelas, and Don D. Jackson (1967), *one cannot not communicate* (p. 49). However, he went on to say, in no language does a double positive ever mean a negative. At this point, from the back of the room, a loud voice could be heard to utter: *yeah, yeah!*

The joke is an apt demonstration of the difference between language and mathematics as symbol systems. And, of course, the joke works best when delivered orally; when read silently it requires that the reader fill in the missing tone of voice, one that indicates a sarcastic response. Admittedly, in a technical sense the meaning here is not conveyed purely via language, but also through the addition of paralanguage, functioning as a form of metalanguage, that is, instructions on how to interpret the meaning of the words. Vocalics such as tone of voice are considered a form of *non*verbal communication, a fact that is often overlooked due to the strong association of nonverbal expression with body language and other visual cues—we frequently give short shrift to the acoustic and *focus* our attention almost entirely on the sense of sight. Another source of confusion has to do with the term *verbal*, which the dictionary defines as *of, relating to, or consisting of words*, but which in popular usage is often equated with the spoken word; by way of contrast, *paralanguage* refers to everything related to speech (and writing) except for words. I should also note the distinction between the general semantics concept of the *non-verbal* (with a hyphen), which refers to forms of pre-linguistic and non-linguistic perception, to thought and sense perception absent the inner monologue that assigns names and explanations to our experience, and the *nonverbal* (without the hyphen) in fields such as communication, anthropology, and psychology, which refers to forms of expression such as kinesics, proxemics, and paralanguage, and to all of the ways that we interact with others apart from our use of words. The two are separate and distinct phenomena, albeit not entirely unrelated.

All joking aside, the twin *nots* in this book's title are consistent with the negative flavor that is characteristic of general semantics. By this I do not mean to refer to individuals with sour dispositions or defensive responses to criticism, as individuals of that sort can be found in every human field, sector, group, and locus of activity. No, what I am referring to is the liberal use of negation in numerous general semantics formulations, including

- the identification of general semantics as a *non*-aristotelian system
- the linking of the *non*-aristotelian to *non*-newtonian physics, *non*-euclidean geometry, and *non*-chrysippian logic
- the fundamental general semantics principle of *non*-identity
- the related principle of *non*-allness
- the holistic concept of *non*-elementalism
- the *non*-linear concept of the *non*-additive
- references to the *non-verbal* or silent level of abstracting
- the frequently invoked saying that "the map is *not* the territory"
- and the companion adage that "the word is *not* the thing"
- as well as Korzybski's (1933/2023) statement that "whatever one might *say* something *'is', it is not*" (p. 409)
- etc.

And then there is the clarification we often need to make about the name *general semantics*, when introducing the discipline to individuals who are unfamiliar with it—that general semantics is *not* semantics.

Semantics, as opposed to general semantics, is about the meaning of words, as in dictionary definitions. This brings to mind another of my favorite linguistics jokes. In this case, a famous linguistic scholar has died, and his colleagues are present at his funeral (whether the deceased is the scholar from the previous joke I cannot say, but if he was, it may be that he died of embarrassment). The widow delivers a eulogy and then asks if anyone else would like to say a word, at which point one of his colleagues steps up to the podium and says, *plethora*. He then returns to his seat. The widow, with a grateful expression on her face, says to him, *that means a lot*.

To be sure, the choices we make regarding definitions are no joke, and can have profound implications. The definitions we give to words such as *life* and *death*, for example, have serious implications that impact medical and political decisions regarding abortion, contraception, in vitro fertilization, artificial life support, cardiopulmonary resuscitation, and euthanasia. Anyone who discounts the different ways in which we define our terms, or dismisses such concerns as *mere semantics*, is making a grave error. And within the discipline of general semantics we do not dismiss the importance of plain old semantics. Indeed, we recognize and try to raise awareness of the fact that definitions are not handed down to us from on high, but rather are human inventions. For this reason, every dictionary definition is subject to debate and disputation, endlessly emendable and open to alternatives, and therefore potentially the source of conflict and negotiation, as George Orwell noted long ago (1946). And as Postman (1995) explains, instead of asking for *the* definition of a word, we ought to ask, in more modest fashion, for *a* definition of a word instead, as no one definition can be truly said to be definitive. Understanding that there can only be *a* definition of a word, that there cannot be *the* definition in any absolute sense, does not necessarily require a shift to the opposite extreme of absolute relativism. No, this is not to suggest that any given definition is just as good as any other. Instead, we can evaluate the usefulness of definitions by how clear and specific they are. In general semantics, the use of definitions that are specific and concrete, operational definitions for example, is encouraged as a means of mitigating some of the difficulties that language presents us with (Johnson, 1946; Postman, 1976). It is also worth noting, to return to the subject of negation, that every definition is also a delimitation, and that every definition, in stating what a term refers to, also implies what the term does not refer to. Put another way, as a product of the abstracting process, every definition sets up a category whose boundaries determine what concepts or phenomena are to be included within the category and what concepts or phenomena are to be excluded.

And to return to the theme of the negative, and the point that general semantics is *not* plain old (but never *mere*) semantics, general semantics is not about meaning in the sense of dictionary definitions, but rather about meaning in general, about meaning-making, the activity that scholars such as Christine Nystrom (2021, 2022) place at the center of human life. Meaning as the ways in which we (and all forms of life) respond to stimuli, external stimuli coming from the environment and other entities within the environment, and internal stimuli coming from our own nervous systems and bodily functions. As a discipline, general semantics focuses on how we know what we know and how we relate to our environment and ourselves; how we interpret and evaluate our surroundings and our own thoughts, feelings, and behavior; how we understand and to a degree construct our reality. Put another way, it is about how we *mediate* with the world, with others, and with ourselves. It is an applied epistemology that includes strategies for critical thinking and clearer communication. The essays collected in *Not A, Not Be, &c* does not require prior familiarity with general semantics, although those with knowledge of the discipline will hopefully find the book rewarding as it seeks to expand the horizons of this tradition. But those new to this non-aristotelian system will, again hopefully, find all terms and concepts adequately explained, and will gain enough of a taste of general semantics to merit further exploration and education.

Having broached the (often uncomfortable) subject of death, albeit in humorous fashion in the joke about the linguist's funeral, I should acknowledge that death represents the ultimate negation, at least from the point of view of individual consciousness. As I have previously noted (Strate, 2011b), our inability to fully come to terms with death is related to the fact that we cannot truly step outside of the system of our own consciousness, however much we might try to imagine it, and no matter the extent to which we observe or acknowledge the death of others. The full and absolute negation of one's own self is unimaginable except in the abstract, however much the abnegation of ego may be a goal in certain spiritual and philosophical systems. At the same time, however, as human beings we are the only form of life capable of becoming aware of our own mortality, so that death constitutes a symbolic black hole that warps the individual and collective human psyche. We become cognizant of the eventuality of our demise as part of the maturation process; it is a development that comes well after language acquisition, as a consequence of our unique capacity for symbolic communication. Ernest Becker (1971) argues that the realization that we are not immortal, that our days are numbered, is so drastic a blow to the ego that the main function of human cultures and religions is to mitigate if not alleviate the trauma by finding ways to engage in the denial of death (e.g., belief in life after death, resurrection, reincarnation, etc.), and/or otherwise providing individuals with a heroic role to play that will be celebrated by those who follow after us. General semantics scholar and media ecologist Corey Anton addresses the need to come to terms with our limited lifespan and inevitable end in his book, *How Non-Being Haunts Being: On Possibilities, Morality, and Death Acceptance* (2020), viewing it in positive terms, and thereby engaging in an effort to negate the negativity of personal negation. In contrast to the binary opposition between being and nothingness (general semantics suggests caution when dealing with two-valued orientations, looking to alternatives via multi-valued orientations instead), Anton, like Sartre (2003), is concerned with being *and* nothingness, or to use one of Korzybski's (1933/2023) extensional devices, *being-nothingness* as a single, inseparable, non-elementalistic or holistic concept, along with *life-death*. Or, to acknowledge the asymmetrical nature of the pairings, being is the *medium* (or *environment*) out of which nothingness emerges, and life is the *medium* (or *environment*) out of which death emerges (Strate, 2017b).

Death awareness gives added impetus to our efforts at time-binding, as we communicate what we know to others, thereby passing knowledge down from one generation to the next. In preserving what has been gained through hard won experience, we are able to, as the saying goes, see further because we are standing on the shoulders of giants, and benefit from the labor of countless human beings who came before us, and are no longer alive (Korzybski, 1921, 1950, 1933/2023). Time-binding begins with capacity for symbolic communication, especially via language and speech, which enables us to encode experience in a form that can be passed on to others. As a social species, the foundation of time-binding is collective memory, which then is supplemented (and to a degree supplanted) through additional storage media, notably through the use of writing, later printing, and more recently electronic technologies. In this way, we are able to make progress, so that our quality of life and life chances have in many ways improved over the course of human history, and pre-history.

Time-binding, I hasten to add also involves a form of negation. It is not simply the positive acquisition and accumulation of knowledge, but also involves the negative function of eliminating errors and inaccuracies. In science and engineering, sectors where human progress is extraordinarily visible, an emphasis on reality-testing and the identification and elimination of whatever turns out to be mistaken and false is essential. For this reason, Korzybski looked to the empirical method for ways in which to improve the human condition more generally. This also means abandoning the age-old quest for absolute truth, in favor of tentative conclusions that are subject to repeated testing. Karl Popper (2002) argues that scientific theories and hypotheses can never be proven true, for the simple reason that for any generalization to be proven absolutely true, we must have access to every specific instance it refers to, every instance that ever was and every instance that ever will be, a practical impossibility. But it only takes one specific instance to prove the generalization false, just one disconfirming instance to demonstrate that the theory or hypothesis is wrong. Therefore, science ultimately depends on the process of testing and falsification, and statements that cannot be falsified are not considered valid scientific generalizations as they are immune from empirical testing (e.g., that God created the world); we move forward with the realization that human beings are fallible, absolute knowledge is unattainable, and that human progress is based on the reduction or elimination of error (otherwise known as addition by subtraction).

Negation as a mean of correcting error is also inherent in the concept of information as put forth by Claude Shannon in his formulation of information theory, (Shannon & Weaver, 1949). Within a code or any set of possible outcomes, states, quantities, or signs, the function of information is to eliminate uncertainty by reducing the number of possibilities, alternatives, or choices. For example, if you have 8 possibilities, reducing them by half to 4, by half again to 2, and by half again to 1 takes us from a degree of uncertainty to one of certainty, each reduction representing one bit of information, easily represented via binary code. It follows that rather than being defined in positive terms, information can be understood as knowledge that the receiver does *not* have about what is coming next in a series of signals or messages, the receiver being a human being, other form of life, a machine, or any other receptacle. This negative function of information is why the concept of information is intimately associated with control, hence Norbert Wiener's (1950, 1961) declaration that *communication is control*. And the science of control, otherwise known as *cybernetics*, as described by Wiener (1950, 1961) depends on the ability of systems to be regulated or regulate themselves via feedback, in effect sending messages that say stop or go, off or on, no or yes (in binary code, zero or one); Gregory Bateson (1972, 1979) emphasized the importance of negative feedback in particular, the imposition of constraints as the means of defining and directing developments, for example pointing to evolution via natural selection as being based on negative feedback that the environment provides to lifeforms (positive feedback on the other hand can result in runaway systems, as in a snowball or butterfly effect).

While negative feedback as a function does play a role in the biophysical environment, negation itself has no physical or material existence, apart from the arbitrary designation of certain energy states and particles as "positive" or "negative" (which only indicates that they are, in a sense, mutually negating). The negative is not an object or artifact, not a *thing*. We can recognize negation as a concept only because we have the words for it. Which is to say that the concept of the negative itself is a function of our ability to engage in symbolic communication, the same ability that grants us the capacity for time-binding. The rhetorician Kenneth Burke (1966) highlights the relationship between language and negation in his essay entitled "Definition of Man"—his attempt to construct a definition of what it means to be a human being, resulting in the following:

> Man is
> the symbol-using (symbol-making, symbol-misusing) animal
> inventor of the negative (or moralized by the negative)

> separated from his natural condition by instruments of his own making
> goaded by the spirit of hierarchy (or moved by the sense of order)
> and rotten with perfection. (p. 16)

Burke was heavily influenced by Korzybski and general semantics, albeit often resulting in a contrary or negative response. For example, Korzybski (1933/2023) argues that the structure of language leads us to make the mistake of imposing identity relationships on reality—the idea basic for Aristotle's logic that one thing can be equal to another, that A=A, one snowflake is equal to another, one tree is equal to another, one person is equal to another, etc.—whereas nothing is absolutely identical to anything else in nature. Burke (1950), on the other hand, takes the contrarian but not incompatible position that identification is intrinsic to symbolic communication and can be understood as the basis of all human communication or rhetoric. According to Burke, for communication to occur, there must be a degree of common ground from which the meaning of a symbolic act is identified and related; through empathy and understanding, the agents participating in communication increase their common ground and thereby their identification with one another. Rather than contradicting one another, these views strike me as two sides of the same coin. The common ground that Burke (1966) shares with Korzybski is readily apparent in his definition, insofar as he identifies language and symbolic communication as the fundamental characteristic of our species. And with the addition of the second clause, he identifies one of the most important consequences of our symbol-using, symbol-making, and symbol-misusing, which he further discusses:

> I am not wholly happy with the word, "inventor." For we could not properly say that man "invented" the negative unless we can also say that man is the "inventor" of language itself. So far as sheerly empirical development is concerned, it might be

> more accurate to say that language and the negative 'invented' man. In any case, we are here concerned with the fact that there are no negatives in nature, and that this ingenious addition to the universe is solely a product of human symbol systems. In an age when we are told, even in song, to "accentuate the positive," and when some experts in verbalization make big money writing inspirational works that praise "the power of positive thinking," the second clause of my definition must take on the difficult and thankless task of celebrating that peculiarly human marvel, the negative. (p. 9)

Burke goes on to note the presence of both the *scientistic* form of propositional negatives, conveyed by statements such as *it is not* ..., and the *dramatistic* form of hortatory negatives, conveyed by commands such as *thou shalt not* ..., hence his parenthetical comment about us being moralized by the negative. The term *scientistic* here refers to the rhetoric of science, the presence of scientific language, whether used appropriately or not; *scientism* therefore can sometimes take on negative connotations (see, for example, Postman, 1992), and certainly deserves to be criticized, as in notions such as *creation science* or the use of statistics in advertisements. In its emphasis on the propositional, that is, statements that can be evaluated empiricially, general semantics would fall under the heading of scientism, as would works such as Alfred North Whitehead and Bertrand Russell's *Principia Mathematica* (1925–1927), and Ludwig Wittgenstein's, *Tractatus Logico-Philosophicus* (1961). As for the term *dramatistic*, it is based on Burke's (1945) perspective on language and rhetoric as a form of symbolic action, acts that are performed by actors or agents, and is related to the symbolic interactionism associated with theorists such as George Herbert Mead (1934), H.D. Duncan (1962, 1968), and Erving Goffman (1959). Here too, rather than seeing these two views as being at odds with one another, I would suggest that they can better be understood as complementary.

Burke favors the dramatistic over the scientistic, and his interest in and sympathy for religion leads him to stress the hortatory function of negation. Certainly, morality and ethics have much to do with a sense of restraint, discipline, and self-control, in other words the ability to say no to ourselves as well as to others. It is important to differentiate between the symbolic value of the negative and the use of *No!* as an exclamation in nonlinguistic and prelinguistic contexts, that is, with pets and infants for example. In such situations, meaning is conveyed not by language, but by paralanguage, which is to say by tone of voice more or less exclusively, sometimes supplemented by nonverbal cues such as gesture, posture, and facial expression. Tone of voice communicates emotion and authority, the spirit of hierarchy that Burke says we are goaded by, and which is dramatistic in nature, although hierarchical relationships exist independently of symbol-use among all social species. But for the toddler on the cusp of language acquisition, learning the meaning of *no*, understanding the concept, represents a major breakthrough in development. Arguably, it is the key breakthrough in acquiring the ability to speak, and think with words, as witnessed by the sudden burst of negation initiated by the child. The point at which children begin to verbalize the negative, when they start to go around saying *No! No! No!*, represents their true entry into the symbolic world. In a sense, this is the point when the young *homo sapiens* first becomes fully human, or if you prefer, takes the first step towards becoming fully human, or towards the ultimate goal of becoming a mature adult. The development begins with the dramatistic, and may also end there. Or it may proceed to the higher level of the scientistic.

In contrast to the prescriptive nature of the hortatory negative, the propositional negative is essentially descriptive. But what exactly does it describe? Significantly, as Burke points out, the negative is unnatural, it does not exist in the physical environment, for, as Aristotle put it, *nature abhors a vacuum*. And as Bateson (1972, 1979) relates, it is only in the symbolic realm that negation not only gains a sense of reality, but has real world consequences, as can be the case for the letter we do not send, the call we do not return, the taxes we do not file, the summons we do not obey, etc. Apart from not being present in the physical universe, absence cannot even be depicted in images, as there is no way of painting or drawing or photographing something that is *not* here, there, or anywhere, and there is no semblance or resemblance of nothingness that can be pictured. Every image must show something, even the blank canvas has color and texture, as 20th century abstract artists aptly demonstrated. This also applies to the mind's eye, how language interacts with imagination, as George Lakoff (2004) explains:

> When I teach the study of framing at Berkeley, in Cognitive Science 101, the first thing I do is I give my students an exercise. The exercise is: Don't think of an elephant! Whatever you do, do not think of an elephant. I've never found a student who is able to do this. Every word, like *elephant*, evokes a frame, which can be an image or other kinds of knowledge: Elephants are large, have floppy ears and a trunk, are associated with circuses, and so on. The word is defined relative to that frame. When we negate a frame, we evoke the frame. (p. 3)

Simply put, it is impossible to respond to the command not to think of an elephant except by thinking of an elephant, which means picturing an elephant (the picture being the basis of the frame that Lakoff refers to—there is no way to create or summon up an image of *not-elephant* in and of itself). There is no way to picture the negative, as it is primarily communicated by words, and visually by abstract marks such as the numeral 0 or the icon of a circle with a slash across it, ⊘, which does not in any way resemble an actual "thing" such as a void or nothingness. Susanne Langer (1957) argues persuasively that images and other forms of presentational symbolism or analogical codes do not have the capacity to form propositions, statements that can be determined true or false (or generalizations that can be falsified); this stands in contrast to language and similar forms of digital codes such as mathematics (see also Nystrom, 2021). And if images on their own cannot form propositional messages, neither can they form propositions expressing negation.

Ultimately, the propositional negative, and by extension the negative in general, represents a highly abstract concept. The process of abstracting, as described by Korzybski (1933/2023), begins with perception, so that percepts are about the most concrete level we can obtain. Images involve a degree of abstracting beyond direct perception, but depictions are still quite concrete, and consequently not propositional. Names that we give to percepts, and descriptions of them that we provide are the lowest form of abstracting, and therefore our most concrete use of language. To use the designation of *elephant*, and to use a description (gray skin, tusks, trunk, large body, etc.) can be very specific. But to say that something is *not* an elephant, or to say that there is *no* elephant here, does not make reference to any specific or actual percept or phenomenon, but rather invokes the entire category that the term *elephant* represents. Put another way, saying, *yes the banana is gone, I ate it*, is a reference to a specific banana, while saying, *yes we have no bananas*, is not about any one identifiable banana, but about any and all bananas, bananas in general, bananas as an abstract category. As Brian Rotman explains in his brilliant little book, *Signifying Nothing: The Semiotics of Zero* (1987), the negative invokes a meta level. Zero for example represents not just a *sign* representing a specific quantity, but a *meta-sign* representing the absence of any quantity or numerical value. Insofar as it stands for the null set, the zero points to the set in its entirety rather than focusing attention solely on a member of the set; it points to the system beyond its individual parts, to the category beyond its individual members. Rotman extends his analysis from the Hindu invention of zero to the advent of the vanishing point in European Renaissance art, and the introduction of imaginary money in the form of paper bills, as related developments. But we can extrapolate backwards as well to understand that negation in language, the simple speech act of just saying *no*, is intimately related to our capacity for abstract thought, and to the abstracting process that human beings are heir to.

I have endeavored here, admittedly in cursory fashion, to make it clear that there is, in fact, nothing negative about negativity, and to explain the importance of negation as it is fundamentally associated with language and symbolic communication, the basic human capacity for abstracting and the ability to engage in higher levels of abstract thinking, our sense of morality and ethics, our ability to form testable propositions, our ability to work on a meta level, our awareness of our own mortality, and our ability to recognize the function of negation in nature despite its lack of physical manifestations. Understanding the enormous value of negation hopefully serves to justify the negative flavor present in general semantics, and the doubling down of negativity in the title I have chosen for this book, *Not A, Not Be, &c.* I do hope that in this instance two negatives result in a positive.

I realize that all of this discussion of negation may leave me open to the accusation of being, to invoke an agnewism from my youth, one of those *nattering nabobs of negativity*. If so, I accept it as a badge of honor. And I would counter with the George Bernard Shaw quote that was often attributed to Robert F. Kennedy back in the 60s: "Some men see things as they are and ask, 'Why?' I dream things that never were and ask, 'Why not?'" Such was the spirit that moved Korzybski in his attempt to develop a means by which we might move past the irrationality of war, violence, oppression, prejudice, and all of the other self-inflicted harms that human beings impose upon themselves. This, for me and for many others, continues to be the motivation behind our work in general semantics, media ecology, and other non-aristotelian systems and approaches.

In a more modest way, in asking the question *why not?*, and otherwise being mindful of the negative theme invoked here, I decided to accede to a contrarian impulse with a somewhat more radical departure, and perform a kind of reversal of the overheated print medium by moving the index and bibliography to the front of the book. Why, after all, are these sections universally relegated to the nether regions of every publication, as if they were nothing more than an appendix, a vestigial organ of no real relevance? Is it anything more than custom that accounts for their placement as a postscript? As far as I am concerned, whenever I am examining a work of nonfiction and considering whether it is worth my while, the first thing that I do is turn to the back of the book to look at what is listed in the index, and what references are consulted in the work, as this tells me more about the book than any blurb on the back cover or any random perusal of its pages. So why not, at least this once, start off with the index (or indices in this case) and works cited, following the front matter? Indeed, given the general semantics concept of time-binding, situating the bibliography at the start acknowledges the work that has come before this one, the work that serves as a foundation upon which this book is built. Admittedly, this reversal also allows me to end the book in a way that I find appealing, and that I hope you will appreciate. In any event, I invite you to look through the list of works cited and topics covered before proceeding on to the six essays collected in this volume, which are divided into three sections.

The first section invokes the *Not A* theme of this book, as the lead essay begins with the concept of the *non-aristotelian*, also contextualizing and complementing general semantics by way of media ecology, and following Korzybski's lead by grounding it all in physics (and a bit of metaphysics). Appearing in print for the first time, "If Not A, Then E" originated as an address at the New Languages, New Relations, New Realities Symposium sponsored by the Institute of General Semantics at Fordham University in New York City in 2010, with subsequent versions presented at the 69th annual New York State Communication Association Conference in 2011; the International Conference on Strategic Communication at Benemérita Universidad Autónoma de Puebla, in Puebla, Mexico in 2012, and as a keynote address at the 14th Annual Convention of the Media Ecology Association, held at Grand Valley State University in Grand Rapids, Michigan in 2013. In addition to the MEA keynote, a studio recording with visuals based on my PowerPoint presentation and my own voiceover was produced at Saint Mary's College of California in 2017 and shared on YouTube. Needless to say (but I will go ahead and say it anyway), the version included in this book represents the definitive and final version of the text.

The second essay in this volume relates to the non-aristotelian principle of non-identity, as it reviews the differences between the three different types of codes or symbol systems: language, images, and numbers/numerals. Simply put, "Word, Image, and Number" considers how language is *not* the same as images or mathematics, images are *not* the same as language or mathematics, and mathematics is *not* the same as language or images. Originating as a series of commissioned blog posts I wrote for the *Visible Works Design Blog* in 2014 and 2015 (which is no longer online), a series that was discontinued before it was completed, I have revised the original versions and added three new sections to finally complete the set.

The second section is devoted to the theme of *Not Be*, and features an extended discussion of the problematic nature of the word *is* and the verb *to be* that Korzybski (1933/2024) originally flagged, and that morphed into efforts to eliminate the verb altogether from our writing, and our speech. "It Is What It Isn't" covers the controversy over the copula, reviews the case against the verb "to be" in general semantics and beyond and before Korzybski, and considers the broader context by way of linguistics and orality-literacy studies. Portions of this study were presented as papers at 22nd Annual Media Ecology Association Convention held online in 2021, at the Science, Sanity, and the Semantic Environment Symposium sponsored by the Institute of General Semantics in New York City in 2021, and more fully as a lecture delivered as part of the online lecture series sponsored by the Institute of General Semantics in 2022, before being published in *ETC: A Review of General Semantics* in 2023 under the title, "The Issue of *Is*: A Commentary on the Case Against the Verb 'To Be'"; the version included in this volume is a revised version of the *ETC* article.

The longest piece in this collection is followed by the shortest one, a reflection entitled "Figments of a Fragment, or Fragments of a Figment," which was originally written at the request of Mark Riva, and published in the inaugural issue of his online magazine *Imagine*, and reprinted in *ETC* in 2024.

The third section represents the *&c* theme of this book, and the fourth essay I have chosen to include originated as a keynote address delivered at the SOCON Social Media Conference, in Atlantic City, New Jersey, in 2014. "So You Want to Change the World? A Hitchhiker's Guide to Subversive Thinking" combines concepts derived from general semantics and media ecology, the title serving as nod to the Douglas Adams stories that began with *The Hitchhiker's Guide to the Galaxy*, and to the classic work on education by Neil Postman and Charles Weingartner, *Teaching as a Subversive Activity* (1969). A print version of the address was published in *Anekaant: A Journal of Polysemic Thought*, the journal of the Balvant Parekh Centre for General Semantics and Other Human Sciences in 2016, and a revised version was delivered as part of the online lecture series sponsored by the Institute of General Semantics in 2023, before being further revised for this volume.

The final essay specifically invokes the theme of *&c* (which is otherwise present throughout the book), as it reviews the extensional devices that Korzybski (1933/2024) originally offered as general semantics correctives for ways in which language can mislead us about the nature of reality. Wendell Johnson (1946) added a number of new devices to Korzybski's list, and in "The And" I offer one more that is closely related to the dear old *et cetera* that e.e. cummings waxed poetically about. Here again, I have incorporated some modest references to linguistics and orality-literacy studies with the intention of enhancing the discussion. This piece was originally presented at the Ecologies of Mind, Media, and Meaning II Online Symposium sponsored by the Institute of General Semantics in 2023, and was published in *ETC: A Review of General Semantics* that same year.

This book represents the third such volume that I have prepared for the Institute of General Semantics, following *On the Binding Biases of Time and Other Essays on General Semantics and Media Ecology* (Strate, 2011b), and *Concerning Communication: Epic Quests and*

Lyric Excursions Within the Human Lifeworld (2022). Like the previous two, this book is donated to the Institute, in that I take no royalties nor monetary compensation for its publication and sale (this is also true of the collection of my poetry, *Diatribal Writes of Passage in a World of Wintertextuality: Poems on Language, Media, and Life (But Not as We Know It)* that the IGS published in 2020). In these three collections of essays, my aim has been consistent: to contribute to the discipline of general semantics and our understanding of the non-aristotelian approach that Korzybski referenced, and to fulfill Postman's call for a general semantics writ large by integrating the tradition associated with Korzbyski, Hayakawa, Johnson, and others with related approaches such as systems theory, communication theory, and media ecology. I therefore also intend to provide something of value to these other areas of study and practice, as I hope I have with previous works, such as *Amazing Ourselves to Death: Neil Postman's Brave New World Revisited* (Strate, 2014), and *Media Ecology: An Approach to Understanding the Human Condition* (2017b). This is not to say that this volume is nothing more than old wine in new bottles. No, this is an original collection, one that includes previously unpublished work, as well as material that has received only limited distribution, in a format that is a bit different from what is typically found in books of this sort. Like the vastly more experimental works produced by Jerome Agel (e.g., Fuller, 1970; McLuhan & Fiore, 1967, 1968), I hope that this departure from standard formatting will assist readers in thinking about the book as a medium, its structure being a matter of somewhat arbitrary human conventions, a construction rather than something "natural" and inevitable, a form that is the product of the process of abstracting as it has occurred over the long history of the written word.

Acknowledgements

In addition to the basic non-aristotelian principle of non-identity, that there are no identity relationships in nature, general semantics includes the principle of non-allness, that we can never know it all, and we can never say all there is to say about anything. It follows that I cannot possibly acknowledge everyone I ought to acknowledge for making this book possible. I therefore apologize for all of my inevitable sins of omission, but will proceed as best I can.

To begin, I am grateful to the Institute of General Semantics, to IGS Vice-President Corey Anton, the editor of the book series this volume is a part of, and to my fellow Trustees, Eva Berger, Thom Gencarelli, Marty Levinson, Jackie Rudig, Dom Heffer, Susan Drucker, Laura Trujillo Liñan, Nora Bateson, Chris Mayer, and Gina Valenti, and to the late Allen Flagg, who first brought me into the IGS community. I also want to include a word of thanks to my New York Society for General Semantics friends, Terry Manzella, Peggy Cassidy, TC McLuhan, and Michelle Shocked. And I want to add my appreciation for my Media Ecology Association associates, including Robert Albrecht, Adriana Braga, Fernando Gutiérrez, Paul Soukup, Heather Stassen, Jacqueline McLeod Rogers, Tiffany Gilliam, Michael Plugh, Matt Thomas, Julia Hildebrand, Jeff Bogaczyk, and Austin Hestdalen. My colleagues at Fordham University deserve a mention as well, including Paul Levinson, Sharif Mowlabocus, Lewis Freeman, Brandy Monk-Payton, Jennifer Moormon, Michele Prettyman, Frank Lo Buono, Heidi Bordogna, and Diana Kamin, and the rest of the faculty, as well as Michelle O'Dwyer and Marie Trombetta. And I want to express my gratitude to my colleagues at NeoPoiesis Press, including Stephen Roxborough, and especially editor-in-chief Dale Winslow, who published two volumes of my poetry, *Thunder at Darwin Station* (2015), and *First Letter of My Alphabet* (2023), as well as the groundbreaking work by Marshall and Eric McLuhan, *Media and Formal Cause* (2011).

In the spirit of time-binding, I would like to acknowledge the enormous debt I owe to my teachers and mentors, from my undergraduate professors Jack Barwind and Njoku Awa to my PhD mentors Neil Postman, Christine Nystrom, and Terry Moran. And a special thank you to another great mentor, Gary Gumpert. And I am grateful to Rabbi Barry Schwartz, to Congregation Adas Emuno, and to Cantor Iris Karlin as well.

Many other names come to mind, and so I would like to express my appreciation for acts both great and small—or for no particular reason—to Lera Boroditsky, Bini B.S., Heather Crandall, Peter Darnell, Kasia Drogowska, Donna Flayhan, Marty Friedman, Noura Hajjaj, Octavio Islas, Susan Jasko, Mary Kahl, Prafulla Kar, Christy Knopf, Igor Korolyov, Michelle Kramisen, KrisTen, Paul Lippert, Jermaine Martinez, Joshua Meyrowitz, Stephen Nachmanovich, Allison Peiritsch, Valerie Peterson, Mark Riva, Amanda Sevilla, Devkumar Trivedi, Ed Wachtel, and Maryanne Wolf.

Lauren Rowland has once again come to my rescue with her enormous artistic talent, providing the cartoons and e-world and tree of life images for this volume, as well as the colorful version of the IGS logo, based on an original design by Valerie Peterson, one that was earlier finalized by Peter Darnell. The image of planet Earth is provided courtesy of the National Aeronautics and Space Administration of the United States government (nasa.gov). And thanks go to Daniel Middleton and Scribe Freelance for their exceptional design work.

And last but never least, I am grateful for the love and support of my family, my wife Barbara, my son Benjamin, and my daughter Sarah.

Index of **Proper Names**

A

Adam, 100
Adams, Douglas, 21, 149, 159
Allen, Woody, 71
Ampère, André-Marie, 50
Anaxagoras, 49
Anaximander, 49
Anaximenes, 49
Anekaant: A Journal of Polysemic Thought, 21
Anton, Corey, i, 10, 23, 33, 39, 55
Arendt, Hannah, 33, 62, 150
Aristotle, 13, 15, 33, 43–47, 49, 52, 55, 64, 95; see also aristotelian
Augustine, 33, 126–127, 132

B

Balvant Parekh Centre, 3, 21
Bardini, Thierry, 33, 152
Baron-Cohen, Simon, 33, 57
Bateson, Gregory, 3, 12, 15, 33, 45, 58, 69, 91, 108, 143, 179
Bateson, Nora, 23, 33
Bavelas, Janet Beavin, , 4, 39, 58, 91
Beauvoir, Simone de, 33, 60
Becker, Ernest, 9, 33
Benemérita Universidad Autónoma de Puebla, 19
Beniger, James R., 33, 84
Berne, Eric, 33, 98

Bertalanffy, Ludwig von, 3, 33, 96
Blake, William, 97, 131
Bolter, Jay David, 33, 159
Boole, George, 44; see also Boolean logic
Boorstin, Daniel J., 33, 84
Boroditsky, Lera, 24, 33, 110, 152
Bourland, David D., Jr., 33–34, 115–117, 120
Buber, Martin, 34, 57
Buggles, The, 72
Burke, Kenneth, 12–15, 34, 45
Burns, Robert, 112

C

Carpenter, Edmund, 34, 47, 83, 163
Carr, Nicholas, 34, 152
Carroll, Lewis, 102
Cassady, Neal, 126
Clinton, Bill, 92
Clinton, Hillary, 155
Condon, John C., Jr., 34, 81, 103
Cooper, David A., 34, 54

D

Day, Doris, 91
Deacon, Terrence W., 34, 55
De Morgan, Augustus, 34, 115–116
Duncan, Hugh Dalziel, 14, 34, 57

E

Edison, Thomas Alva, 50
Einstein, Albert, 34, 50–51, 54, 57, 125, 127, 144, 164, 170
Eisenstein, Elizabeth L., 34, 58, 61, 64, 144, 176
Eliade, Mircea, 34, 61, 130
Elohim, 60–61, 63
Ellis, Albert, 34, 117, 170
Ellul, Jacques, 34–35, 58, 112, 143
Engelbart, Douglas, 152
ETC: A Review of General Semantics, 20–21, 35–37, 39, 117, 169
Evans, Ray, 91
Eve, 64

F

Faraday, Michael, 50
Fenollosa, Ernest, 35, 118
Fiore, Quentin, 22, 36, 58, 141, 164
Fisch, Richard, 39, 58, 128
Fordham University, 1, 19, 23
Franklin, Benjamin, 50, 165
Frith, Uta, 35, 57
Fuller, R. Buckminster, 22, 35, 54

G

Galvani, Luigi, 50
Gandhi, Mahatma, 147
Geddes, Patrick, 148
Gencarelli, Thom, 23, 169
Gleick, James, 35, 53
God, 11, 34, 54, 60, 92, 100, 142, 172–174, 176–177
Goddard, Jean Luc, 103
Gomperz, Theodor, 35, 116
Goffman, Erving, 14, 35, 57, 142
Goody, Jack, 4, 35, 47, 58, 110, 144
Gorgias, 37, 116
Gould, Stephen Jay, 35, 111
Gozzi, Raymond Jr., 35, 112, 156, 158
Grand Valley State University, 19
Gromala, Diane, 33, 159

H

Hall, Edward T., 35, 131
Havelock, Eric A., 4, 35, 47, 58, 121–123, 128–129
Hayakawa, S.I., 22, 35, 44, 57, 93, 169
Hayakawa, A.R., 35, 57
Heinlein, Robert, 133
Heisenberg, Werner, 144
Heraclitus, 36, 49
Herodotus, 123
Hertz, Heinrich, 50
Hesiod, 121–122
Homer, 121–123, 128, 161
Hugo, Victor, 111
Huxley, Aldous, 35, 97

I

Innis, Harold A., 35, 58
Institute of General Semantics, 1–2, 19–22, 23, 36, 39, 103, 117, 168

J

Jackson, Don D., 4, 39, 58, 91
Jobs, Steve, 145, 148, 159
Johnson, Andrea, 35, 117
Johnson, Mark, 36, 112, 156
Johnson, Wendell, 8, 21, 22, 35, 49, 57, 104, 110, 147, 154–155, 162, 170
Johnston, Paul Dennithorne, 34, 117

K

Kaparo, Risa, 35, 118
Kauffman, Stuart, 35, 53

Kay, Alan, 152, 159
Kennedy, Robert F., 26
Kesey, Ken, 126, 132
Kirk, G.S., 36, 49
Klein, Jeremy, 34, 36, 117
Korzybski, Alfred, i, iv, 2–4, 6, 10, 11, 13, 17–22, 36, 43–45, 48–52, 54, 56–57, 59, 62, 68, 93–100, 103, 97, 99–100, 103, 105–107, 111–112, 115–116, 119–120, 123, 125, 128, 133–134. 150, 153–155, 162, 167–170, 173, 179

L

Lady Gaga, 155
Lahman, Mary P., 4, 36
Lakoff, George, 16, 36, 112, 156
Lakoff, Robin T., 36, 119–121, 123–124
Langer, Susanne K., 16, 36, 45, 79–80, 83
Lee, Dorothy, 36, 54. 99–100, 152, 163
Lewinsky, Monica, 93
Livingston, Jay, 91
Logan, Robert K., 33, 36, 39, 47, 55
Lycophron, 116

M

Maas, David F., 36, 117
Marconi, Guglielmo, 50
Maslow, Abraham H., 36, 57
Maturana, Humberto R., 36, 53, 55
Maxwell, James Clerk, 50
McGilchrist, Iain, 36, 80
McLuhan, Eric, 24, 36–37, 55, 58
McLuhan, Marshall, i, 2, 4, 22, 24, 33, 36–37, 39, 46–48, 50–51, 54–55, 58–59, 62, 69–70, 77, 93, 99–101, 141–145, 150–152, 160, 162–164, 175–176
Mead, George Herbert, 14, 37, 57, 109
Mead, Margaret, 148
Media Ecology Association, 1–2, 19–20, 23
Meeker, Joseph W., 37, 149
Merleau-Ponty, Maurice, 37, 60
Molière, 101
Morse, Samuel, 50
Moses, 92, 174
Moses, Robert, 96
Mumford, Lewis, 34, 37, 58, 61,157
Murphy, Cullen, 37, 116

N

New York Society for General Semantics, 1, 23
New York State Communication Association, 2, 19
Nystrom, Christine L., 8, 16, 24, 37, 80, 109, 127

O

Ong, Walter J., 2, 4, 37, 47–48, 54, 57–58, 72, 93, 129, 152, 157, 160, 175–177
Oppenheimer, J. Robert, 98
O'Reilly, Tim, 37, 153–154
Orwell, George, 8, 37, 103

P

Palin, Sarah, 155
Parks, Rosa, 155
Peirce, Charles Sanders, 3, 37, 44
Perkinson, Henry, 37, 55, 84, 111
Philologos, 37, 173–175
Picasso, Pablo, 54, 144

Plato, 35, 37, 121, 123, 128–129, 152
Popeye, 91
Popper, Karl, 11, 37, 108
Postman, Neil, 2–3, 8, 14, 21–22, 24, 37–39, 45, 58, 62, 84–85, 89, 93, 103–104, 109, 111, 143, 150, 155, 158–159, 162, 169

R
Richards, I.A., 38, 44, 103, 179
Rogers, Carl R., 38, 57
Rotman, Brian, 17, 38
Russell, Bertrand, 14, 34, 40, 44, 61, 107

S
Safire, William, 38, 89–90
Saint Mary's College of California, 19
Santayana, George, 38, 115–116
Sapir, Edward, 31, 38, 54, 100, 152
Sartre, Jean-Paul, 10, 38, 60
Schmandt-Besserat, Denise, 38, 47, 58, 111, 163
Sculley, John, 145
Seinfeld, Jerry, 38, 90–91
Shannon, Claude E., 3, 11, 38, 44–45, 53, 144
Shaw, George Bernard, 18
Shelley, Mary, 50
Shlain, Leonard, 38, 51
Small, Gary, 38, 151
Stalin, 84
Stein, Gertrude, 95
Steinberg, S. H., 39, 144
Strate, Lance, 1–2, 3, 9–10, 21–22, 33, 39, 47, 55, 57, 59, 62, 84, 100–104, 112, 117–119, 131, 142, 146, 149, 157, 162, 164, 168, 171
Streep, Meryl, 155

T
Talking Heads, 131
Tannen, Deborah, 39, 58
Tesla, Nikola, 50
Thales, 49
Thompson, J.J., 50
Trujillo Liñán, Laura, i, 23, 39, 55
Turkle, Sherry, 39, 152
Twain, Mark, 111
Twenge, Jean M., 39, 143
Turing, Alan, 144

V
Varela, Francisco J., 36, 53, 55
Vorgan, Gigi, 38, 151

W
Waldrop, M. Mitchell, 39, 53
Watzlawick, Paul, 4, 39, 58, 91, 108, 128
Weakland, John H., 39, 58, 128
Weaver, Warren, 3, 11, 38, 53
Weingartner, Charles, 32, 38, 58, 109, 150, 158
Wiener, Norbert, 3, 12, 39, 45, 144
Whitehead, Alfred North, 14, 40, 44, 107
Whorf, Benjamin Lee, 31, 40, 54, 100, 125, 127, 129–130, 152, 164
Wilden, Anthony, 40, 97
Wilson, Robert Anton, 2, 40, 117
Wittgenstein, Ludwig, 14, 40, 45
Wolf, Maryann, 24, 40, 151
Wolfe, Tom, 40, 126–127

Subject Index

A

abstract, abstracting, abstraction, 6, 8, 9, 16–18, 22, 46–47, 56–57, 59, 68, 74–79, 95, 106–107, 109–111, 116, 122–123, 128–129, 134, 148, 153–155, 167, 170
acoustic, 5, 54, 157, 160–161, 176
advertising, 14, 156
alphabet, 2, 4, 24, 39, 46–49, 64, 129, 144, 151, 157, 176, 178
analog, analogic, analogical, 16, 79–80, 83, 97, 112–113, 153, 175
analysis, 17, 46–47, 84, 98, 152, 157
Aristotelian logic, 47, 54, 95–96, 105–108
art, 16, 17, 24, 36, 37, 38, 51, 61, 72, 83, 84, 98–100, 138, 143, 144, 151, 152, 163
atomism, 46–47, 49, 128
audiovisual, 72, 131

B

bibliography, 18–19
binary code, 12, 75, 158

C

change, 34, 39, 49, 52, 53, 55, 74, 91–92, 97, 102, 108, 128–130, 134, 141, 146, 148, 158, 168–169
chaos, 35, 52, 55, 68, 95
chemistry-binding, 52
clock, 80, 131, 157
codes, 10–12, 16, 20, 29, 68, 74–75, 83, 95, 158
comedy, 37, 38, 90, 122, 149, 160
communication, 1–2, 5–6, 9–10, 12–13, 15, 18–19, 21–22, 34, 35, 38, 39, 46, 52, 57, 59, 68, 71, 80, 85, 122, 134, 144–145, 151–152, 162, 167–168, 179
complexity, 39, 53, 55, 164
computer, 46, 48, 84, 103, 132, 144–145, 152, 158
concrete, 8, 17, 46, 74–77, 83, 104, 107, 109, 118, 123, 128, 147–148, 154, 170
consciousness, 9, 49, 54, 57, 59, 100, 106, 119, 128, 134, 136, 138, 147, 153
context, 15, 19, 20, 46, 74, 82, 84, 104, 109, 118, 133, 162, 168, 170, 179–180
culture, 4, 9, 36, 37, 38, 46, 48, 58, 72, 109, 123, 127, 129–131, 144–145, 149, 159, 161, 163, 170, 172, 175–178
cybernetics, 2–3, 12, 38, 39, 45, 144
cyberspace, 162, 164

D

death, 7, 9–10, 52, 84, 94, 152, 154, 159
definitions, 5, 7, 8, 12, 14, 16, 78–79, 81–82, 89, 93, 95, 103–105, 111–112, 125, 129, 154–155, 169
democracy, 84, 154, 170
digital, 16, 73–75, 77, 79, 83–84, 97, 112, 132, 144–145
discursive, 83
dramatism, 14–15

E

Earth (planet), 24, 64, 92, 131, 176–177
ecology, ecological, 3, 4, 18–19, 21, 22, 33, 38, 39, 45, 55, 58–59, 62, 73, 93, 119, 149, 160, 162, 164, 175
Eden, 64, 130
effects, 12, 55, 91, 115, 119, 120, 136, 146–147, 151
electricity, electric technology, electronic, 10, 48–51, 54–55, 64, 72, 74, 131, 144–145, 149, 151, 159–162, 163, 165
emergence, 10, 55, 109, 136
emotion, 15, 84, 155, 170
empathy, 13, 57–59, 129
empirical method, empiricism, 11, 13–14, 29, 76, 108, 110
energy, 12, 51–55
engineering, 11, 36, 51–52, 95, 143
Enlightenment, 84, 138
entropy, 52–53, 55
environment, 70, 75, 97, 99, 129

E-prime, 33–36, 115–120, 124, 128, 134
equilibrium, 53, 55, 97
etc., 3–4, 21, 60, 115, 169–171
ethics, 15, 18, 50
event, events, 54–57, 59, 69, 91, 94, 97, 107, 121, 125–127, 129–130, 132, 135–137, 164–165, 167–168
evolution, 12, 53, 55, 123, 145, 151, 154, 165
existence, existentialism, 50, 60, 63, 129, 135, 136, 160, 178
experience, 6, 10, 47, 55–59, 61, 68, 70, 73, 83, 97–99, 113, 122, 131–132, 136–138, 159–162
extensional, extensional devices, 3, 10, 21, 102, 133, 167–171, 178–179

F

fallibilism, 11
feedback, 12, 38, 163
film, 69, 71–72, 103, 136
Fordism, 84
frame, 16, 163

G

general semantics, 1–2, 3–4, 6–10, 13, 18–23, 33–36, 38–39, 43–44, 54, 57, 60, 68, 76, 89, 92–93, 96–97, 102–104, 106–107, 109, 112, 115, 117, 120, 133, 141, 150, 167–170
grammar, grammarians, 34, 78, 93, 109, 171, 175

H

homeostasis, 53, 97, 147
hortatory, 14–15
human, humanity, 1–2, 3, 6, 9–15, 17–18, 21–22, 33, 36–37, 39, 46, 48, 52, 55, 57, 59, 62, 72, 80, 82, 90, 94–95, 98, 100, 105–109, 111–112, 126, 132, 148, 151, 155, 158, 160, 162–163, 179

I

icon, 16, 74, 82, 151
identity, 13, 23, 47, 91–92, 94–96, 100–103, 105–106, 109, 112–113, 115, 120, 123–124, 128, 132, 134, 142, 155; see also non-identity
images, 16–17, 20, 67–71, 73–77, 79, 81–85, 157, 163
imagination, 9, 16, 17, 21, 57, 70–73, 118–119, 129, 132, 135–138
index, 18–19, 115, 122, 167–169
individualism, 46, 107, 160
induction, 76
industrialism, industrial revolution, 84, 143, 145
inference, 34, 133, 141
information technology, 84, 153, 157, 162
information theory, 3, 11–12, 44–45, 53, 68, 70, 137, 144
internet, 145, 162
Ionian physicists, 46, 49, 128

K

Kabbalah, 54, 60, 62–63, 147

L

language, 4–6, 8–10, 12–22, 33–35, 37–40, 45–46, 49, 54, 57, 75, 78–79, 81, 83, 89, 92–93, 95, 97, 100–101, 106, 109–110, 112–113, 115–118, 120–121, 123–125, 127–130, 132, 134, 151–152, 155–156, 162, 164, 167, 171, 173–178
linearity, 31, 53, 57, 132–133, 163, 165; see also non-linear
linguistics, 4, 6–7, 9, 15, 20–21, 38, 54, 76, 78, 94, 98–101, 107, 119–120, 123–124, 127, 162, 164, 175
literacy, 20–21, 35, 37, 48, 119, 120–124, 128–132, 144–145, 149, 151, 160–161, 163, 175–178
literature, 37, 83, 163
logic, 6, 13, 34, 37, 43–47, 49, 54, 58, 64, 76, 79, 95–97, 105–108, 115–116, 119, 121, 124, 133, 152, 163, 167, 175

M

map, 6, 54, 68, 92–93, 134, 137, 153–154, 156, 162, 165
mathematics, 5, 16, 20, 38, 40, 67–68, 76, 95, 111
meaning, meaning making, 3–5, 7–8, 13, 15, 38, 47, 68, 72, 74, 77–79, 81–83, 93–94, 96, 103–105, 109, 118, 133–134, 137, 151, 157, 162, 168–171, 175, 179
media, media environment, 9, 10, 21, 48, 51, 54–55, 58–59, 62, 63, 72, 84, 99–100, 109, 131, 144–145, 150–153, 159–162, 164–165, 172

media ecology, 1–2, 3–4, 10, 18–22, 35–39, 45, 55, 73, 93, 119, 150–151, 162, 164, 175
memory, memorization, 10, 121, 126–127, 136–138, 151–153, 176, 178
metacommunication, metalanguage, metasign, 5, 17–18, 102
metaphor, 35–36, 47, 61, 112–113, 118, 153, 156–158, 161–162, 164
morphemes, 78
music videos, 71–72

N

name, naming, 3, 6, 17, 57, 83, 99–103, 112, 154, 156
negative, negation, 4, 6, 8–18, 45, 91, 108
newtonian physics, 43, 51, 54, 161; see also non-newtonian
non-additive, 6, 96
non-allness, 6, 23, 105, 169
non-aristotelian, 3, 6, 9, 22, 23, 43–44, 48, 50, 52, 91, 92, 117, 124–125, 167
non-chrysippian logic, 6
non-contradiction, 47, 105
non-elementalism, 6, 10
non-euclidian, 6, 43, 50, 125
non-identity, 6, 20, 23, 92, 100, 113, 120, 167
non-newtonian, 6, 43, 50, 54, 64, 125
non-linear, nonlinear, 6, 55
non-verbal (level), 6, 57
nonverbal (communication), 5–6, 15, 80, 169–170
novels, 69–70, 149, 158

numbers, numerals, 16—17, 20, 59, 67–69, 73–78, 80, 83–85, 102, 110–111, 155

O

objectivity, 46, 57, 110, 116, 126–127, 123, 160–161
orality, oral culture, 5, 48, 50, 54, 119, 121–123, 128–131, 149, 163, 176–178
orality-literacy studies, 20–21, 37, 119–123, 128, 131, 175

P

paralanguage, 5–6, 15,
perception, 6, 17, 35, 37, 57, 67–68, 73, 77, 80, 97–100, 107, 110, 126, 132, 137, 152, 154
philosophy, 9, 35–36, 45–46, 49, 60, 62, 90, 97, 109, 115–116, 121, 128, 146, 150, 152
phonemes, 78
physics, 6, 19, 38, 43, 50–51, 54, 64, 97–98, 125, 129, 132, 161
picture, 16, 67–69, 71–75, 79, 82–84, 156
presentational, 16, 83
printing, 10, 18–19, 34, 39, 84, 109, 117, 143–144, 149, 151, 161, 170, 172, 176
propaganda, 34, 103
propositional, propositions, 14–18, 83, 116, 119–120
psychotherapy, 38, 57, 98, 117, 170

Q

questions, 18, 83, 104, 121, 158–159, 174, 179

R

radio, 50, 71–73, 144
religion, 9, 15, 37, 60–61, 118, 129, 142, 158, 172
Renaissance, 17, 151

S

sacred, 34, 60, 95, 130–131
Sapir-Whorf Hypothesis, 100
science, 3, 11, 12, 14, 37, 43, 50–52, 61–62, 76, 83–84, 92, 94–96, 98, 101, 104, 110, 144, 150, 160–161, 163, 165
scientific management, 143
scientism, 14–15
self-reflexiveness, 107
semantic reactions, 94–95, 162
semantics, 7–8
semiotics, 3, 17, 37–38, 44
senses, 6, 77, 80, 99–100, 126, 131–132, 137, 151, 160–161
social media, 21, 145, 153
sound, 51, 54, 72, 78, 80–81, 99, 129, 160–161, 176
space, 46, 51, 54, 57, 61, 64, 81, 97, 107, 125, 129, 131, 135, 160, 162–165, 167–168, 170
space-binding, 52
speech, 4–5, 10, 17, 20, 78, 89, 102, 113, 119, 121–122, 127, 129, 151, 170, 176, 179
spirituality, 9, 60, 98
statements, 3, 11, 14, 16, 46, 78–79, 81–83, 95, 100–103, 105–108, 112–113, 115, 119–122, 123, 128, 133–134, 155, 169–170, 178–179
structural differential, 56–57, 107

symbol, symbolic form, symbol systems, symbolic communication, 5, 10, 12–16, 18, 34, 43, 45–46, 49–50, 57, 68–69, 76–77, 92, 94–95, 99, 116, 123, 149, 151, 167, 179
symbolic interactionism, 14, 57
syntax, 78, 122, 171
systems, systems view, systems theory, 3, 12, 17, 22, 33, 45, 52–53, 55, 59–60, 81, 96, 147

T

technology, 10, 34–35, 37–38, 48, 50–51, 54, 58–59, 84, 100, 111–112, 132, 144–146, 153, 157, 159, 162, 164–165,
television, 71–73, 84, 111, 144–145, 162
thermodynamics, laws of, 51–53
time, 4, 46, 51–55, 57, 60, 64, 73, 74, 81, 84, 97, 105, 107, 113, 115, 125–134, 135, 156–157, 160, 164–165, 167–171
time-binding, 4, 10–12, 19, 21–22, 39, 52, 179
translation, 2, 52, 60, 75, 100–101, 124, 161, 169, 172–176, 178
Tree of Life, 62–64
tribal culture, 4, 151, 163
truth, 11, 121, 161
two-valued orientation, 10, 105, 158

V

verbs, 3, 20, 34–35, 54, 92–94, 97, 102–104, 107–109, 112–113, 115–125, 127, 129, 132, 134, 136, 155, 164–165, 175

virtual, 161
vision, visual space, visualism, 5, 16, 46, 47, 54, 67, 70, 71–72, 100, 131, 133, 151, 157, 160–161, 163, 176

W

web, websites, 117, 145, 153–154, 162
word, words, 5–8, 15–16, 20, 46, 47, 60, 67–71, 73, 75–85, 90–91, 92–93, 99–100, 102–105, 109–110, 118, 119, 123, 124, 128–129, 149, 151, 153–155-157, 160–161, 167–171, 175–176, 178

writing, 4–5, 10, 22, 33, 35, 38, 46–47, 76, 78, 84, 110, 117–119, 123, 128–131, 144, 151–153, 157, 161, 162–163, 167–170, 176–178

Y

YouTube, 19

Z

zero, 12, 17, 38, 74–75, 80
zero copula language, 120, 123–124, 128, 132

References

Anton, C. (2020). *How non-being haunts being*. Fairleigh Dickinson University Press.

Anton, C., Logan, R.K., & Strate, L. (2017). *Taking up McLuhan's cause*. Intellect.

Arendt, H. (1958). *The human condition* (2nd ed.). University of Chicago Press.

Arendt, H. (1978). *The life of the mind*. Harvest.

Aristotle. (1998). *The metaphysics* (H. Lawson-Tancred, Trans.). Penguin.

St. Augustine. (1991). *Confessions* (H. Chadwick, Trans.). Oxford University Press.

Bardini, T. (2000). *Bootstrapping*. Stanford University Press.

Baron-Cohen, S. (1995). *Mindblindness: An essay on autism and theory of mind*. MIT Press.

Bateson, G. (1972). *Steps to an ecology of mind*. Bantam Books.

Bateson, G. (1979). *Mind and nature*. Bantam Books.

Bateson, N. (2016). *Small arcs of larger circles*. Triarchy Press.

Bateson, N. (2023). *Combining*. Triarchy Press.

Beauvoir, S. de. (2015). *The second sex*. Vintage Classics.

Becker, E. (1971). *The denial of death*. Free Press.

Beniger, J.R. (1986). *The control revolution*. Harvard University Press.

Berne, E. (1964). *Games people play*. Grove.

Bertalanffy, L.v. (1969). *General system theory*. G. Braziller.

Bolter, J.D. & Gromala, D. (2003). *Windows and mirrors*. MIT Press.

Boorstin, D.J. (1978). *The image*. Atheneum.

Boroditsky, L. (2011, February). How language shapes thought. *Scientific American*, 63–65.

Bourland, D.D., Jr. (1965/1966). A linguistic note: Writing in E-prime. *General Semantics Bulletin 32/33*, 111–114.

Bourland, D. D., & Johnston, P.D. (Eds.). (1991). *To be or not: An E-Prime anthology*. International Society for General Semantics.

Bourland, D. D., & Johnston, P. D. (Eds.). (1997). *E-Prime III: A third anthology*. International Society for General Semantics.

Bourland, D. D., Klein, J., & Johnston, P.D. (Eds.). (1994). *More E-Prime: To be or not II*. International Society for General Semantics.

Buber, M. (1970). *I and thou* (W. Kaufmann, Trans.). Charles Scribner's Sons.

Burke, K. (1945). *A grammar of motives*. University of California Press.

Burke, K. (1950). *A rhetoric of motives*. University of California Press.

Burke, K. (1966). *Language as symbolic action*. University of California Press.

Carpenter, E. (1973). *Oh, what a blow that phantom gave me!* Holt, Rinehart & Winston.

Carr, N. (2010). *The shallows*. W.W. Norton.

Condon, J.C., Jr. (1985). *Semantics and communication* (3rd ed.). Macmillan.

Cooper, D.A. (1997). *God is a verb*. Riverhead Books.

Deacon, T.W. (2012). *Incomplete nature*. W. W. Norton.

De Morgan, A. (1847). *Formal logic or, the calculus of inference, necessary and probable*. Taylor and Walton.

Duncan, H.D. (1962). *Communication and social order*. Bedminster Press.

Duncan, H.D. (1968). *Symbols in society*. Oxford University Press.

Einstein, A., Dewey, J., Jeans, J., Wells, H.G., Dreiser, T., Mencken, H.L., Adams, J.T., Peterkin, J., Keith, A., Babbit, I., Webb, B., Krutch, J.W., Nansen, F., Mumford, L., Millikan, R.A., Shih, H., Belloc, H., Haldane, J.B.S., Nathan, G.J., Edman, I., Russell, B., & Ralphinge, W.. (1931). *Living philosophies*. Simon & Schuster.

Eisenstein, E.L. (1979). *The printing press as an agent of change* (2 vols.). Cambridge University Press.

Eliade, M. (1954). *The myth of the eternal return or, Cosmos and history*. (W.R. Trask, Trans.). Pantheon.

Eliade, M. (1959). *The sacred and the profane* (Willard Trask, Trans.). Harvest/HBJ Books.

Ellis, A. (2001). *Feeling better, getting better, staying better*. Impact.

Ellul, J. (1964). *The technological society* (J. Wilkinson, Trans.). Knopf.

Ellul, J. (1965). *Propaganda* (K. Kellen & J. Lerner, Trans.). Vintage.

Ellul, J. (1980). *The technological system* (J. Neugroschel, Trans.). Continuum.

REFERENCES

Ellul, J. (1985). *The humiliation of the word* (J.M. Hanks, Trans.). Williams B. Eerdmans.

Ellul, J. (1990). *The technological bluff* (G. W. Bromiley, Trans.). Eerdmans.

Fenollosa, E. (2008). *The Chinese character as a medium for poetry.* Fordham University Press.

Frith, U. (1989). *Autism.* Blackwell.

Fuller, R.B. (1963). *No more secondhand god.* Southern Illinois University Press.

Fuller, R.B. (1970). *I seem to be a verb.* Bantam.

Gleick, J. (1987). *Chaos: Making a new science.* Viking Penguin.

Gomperz, T. (1901). *Greek thinkers: A history of ancient philosophy, volume 1* (L Magnus, Trans.). John Murray, Albemarle Street.

Goffman, E. (1959). *The presentation of self in everyday life.* Anchor Books.

Goody, J. (1977). *The domestication of the savage mind.* Cambridge University Press.

Gould, S. J. (1992). *The mismeasure of man.* Penguin Books.

Gozzi, R., Jr. (1999). *The power of metaphor in the age of electronic media.* Hampton Press.

Hall, E.T. (1983). *The dance of life.* Anchor Press.

Havelock, E.A. (1963). *Preface to Plato.* The Belknap Press of Harvard University Press.

Havelock, E.A. (1978). *The Greek concept of justice.* Harvard University Press.

Havelock, E.A. (1982). *The literate revolution in Greece and its cultural consequences.* Princeton University Press.

Havelock, E.A. (1986). *The muse learns to write.* Yale University Press.

Hayakawa, S.I. & Hayakawa, A.R. (1990). *Language in thought and action* (5th ed.). Harcourt Brace.

Huxley, A. (1954). *The doors of perception.* Chatto & Windus.

Innis, H.A. (1951). *The bias of communication.* University of Toronto Press.

Innis, H.A. (1972). *Empire and communication* (rev. ed.). University of Toronto Press.

Johnson, A. (1992). Oh to be a writer. *ETC: A Review of General Semantics 49*(2), 168–170.

Johnson, W. (1946). *People in quandaries.* New York: Harper & Row.

Kaparo, R. (1992). Poetry and E-Prime: Some preliminary thoughts. *ETC: A Review of General Semantics 49*(2), 180–182.

Kauffman, S. (1995). *At home in the universe.* Oxford University Press.

Kirk, G.S. (1954). *Heraclitus: The cosmic fragments.* Cambridge University Press.

Klein, J. (Ed.). (1992). The E-Prime controversy: A symposium [Special Issue]. *ETC: A Review of General Semantics 49*(2).

Korzybski, A. (1921). *Manhood of humanity: The science and art of human engineering.* E. P. Dutton.

Korzybski, A. (1950). *Manhood of humanity: An introduction to non-aristotelian systems and general semantics* (2nd ed.). Institute of General Semantics.

Korzybski, A. (2023). *Science and sanity: An introduction to non-aristotelian systems and general semantics* (6th ed.). Institute of General Semantics. (Original work published 1933)

Lahman, Mary P. (2018). *Awareness and action: A travel companion.* Institute of General Semantics.

Lakoff, G. & Johnson, M. (1980). *Metaphors we live by.* University of Chicago Press.

Lakoff, R.T. (1992). Not ready for prime time. *ETC: A Review of General Semantics 49*(2), 142–145.

Langer, S.K. (1957). *Philosophy in a new key* (3rd ed.). Harvard University Press.

Lee, D. (1959). *Freedom and culture.* Prentice-Hall.

Logan, R.K. (2004). *The alphabet effect.* Hampton Press.

Maas, D.F. (2011). *The new American Standard Bible in E-Prime.* Institute of General Semantics. <https://generalsemantics.org/Applications-of-General-Semantics>

Maslow, A.H. (1954). *Motivation and personality.* Harpers.

Maturana, H.R. & Varela, F.J. (1980). *Autopoiesis and cognition.* D. Reidel.

Maturana, H.R. & Varela, F.J. (1992). *The tree of knowledge* (revised ed., R. Paolucci, Trans.). Shambhala.

McGilchrist, I. (2009). *The master and his emissary.* Yale University Press.

McLuhan, M. (1962). *The Gutenberg galaxy.* University of Toronto Press.

McLuhan, M. (1964). *Understanding media: The extensions of man.* McGraw Hill.

McLuhan, M. (2003). *Understanding me* (S. McLuhan & D. Staines, Eds.). MIT Press.

McLuhan, M. & Fiore, Q. (1967). *The medium is the massage.* Bantam.

McLuhan, M. & Fiore, Q. (1968). *War and peace in the global village.* Bantam.

McLuhan, M. & McLuhan, E. (2011). *Media and formal cause*. NeoPoiesis Press.

Mead, G.H. (1934). *Mind, self and society* (C.W. Morris, Ed.). University of Chicago Press.

Meeker, J. W. (1997). *The comedy of survival* (3rd ed.). University of Arizona Press.

Merleau-Ponty, M. (1962). *Phenomenology of perception*. Routledge & Kegan Paul.

Mumford, L. (1934). *Technics and civilization*. Harcourt Brace.

Mumford, L. (1952). *Art and technics*. Columbia University Press.

Mumford, L. (1961). *The city in history*. Harcourt Brace and World.

Mumford, L. (1967). *The myth of the machine: I. Technics and human development*. Harcourt Brace and World.

Mumford, L. (1970). *The myth of the machine: II. The pentagon of power*. Harcourt Brace Jovanovich.

Murphy, C. (1992, February). "To be" in their bonnets: A matter of semantics. *The Atlantic Monthly*, 18–24.

Nystrom, C.L. (2021). *The genes of culture, Vol. 1*. Peter Lang.

Nystrom, C.L. (2022). *The genes of culture, Vol. 2*. Peter Lang.

Ong, W.J. (1967). *The presence of the word*. Yale University Press.

Ong, W.J. (1969). World as view and world as event. *American Anthropologist 71*(4), 634–647.

Ong, W. J. (1982). *Orality and literacy*. Routledge.

O'Reilly, T. (2017). *WTF: What's the future and why it's up to us*. HarperCollins.

Orwell, G. (1946). Politics and the English language. *Horizon: A Review of Literature and Art 13*(76), 252–265.

Peirce, C.S. (1991). *Peirce on signs: Writings on semiotic*. University of North Carolina Press.

Perkinson, H. (1996). *No safety in numbers*. Hampton Press.

Philologos. (2022, January 26). Why the Bible uses the word "and" so much. *Mosaic*. https://mosaicmagazine.com/observation/religion-holidays/2022/01/why-the-bible-uses-the-word-and-so-much.

Plato. (1971). *Gorgias* (W. Hamilton, Trans.). Penguin.

Popper, K. (2002). *The logic of scientific discovery*. New York: Routledge.

Postman, N. (1968, November 29). Growing up relevant. Address delivered at the 58th annual convention of the National Council of Teachers of English, Milwaukee, WI.

Postman, N. (1970). The reformed English curriculum. In A.C. Eurich (Ed.), *High school 1980: The shape of the future in American secondary education* (pp.160–168). Pitman.
Postman, N. (1974). Media ecology: General semantics in the third millennium. *General Semantics Bulletin 41–43*, 74–78.
Postman, N. (1976). *Crazy talk, stupid talk*. Delacorte.
Postman, N. (1979). *Teaching as a conserving activity*. Delacorte.
Postman, N. (1985). *Amusing ourselves to death*. Viking.
Postman, N. (1988). *Conscientious objections*. Alfred A. Knopf.
Postman, N. (1992). *Technopoly: The surrender of culture to technology*. Alfred A. Knopf.
Postman, N. (1995). *The end of education*. Alfred A. Knopf.
Postman, N. (1999). *Building a bridge to the eighteenth century*. Alfred A. Knopf.
Postman, N. & Weingartner, C. (1966). *Linguistics*. Delta.
Postman, N. & Weingartner, C. (1969). *Teaching as a subversive activity*. Delta.
Richards, I.A. (1952). Communication between men: The meaning of language. In H. Foerster (Ed.), *Transactions of 8th Macy conference: Cybernetics: Circular causal, and feedback mechanisms in biological and social system* (pp. 45–91). Josiah Macy, Jr. Foundation.
Rogers, C.R. (1951). *Client-centered therapy*. Houghton Mifflin.
Rotman, B. (1987). *Signifying nothing: The semiotics of zero*. St. Martin's Press.
Safire, W. (2006, March 5). It is what it is. *New York Times*, 6.22.
Santayana, G. (1923). *Scepticism and animal faith*. Charles Scribner's Sons.
Sapir, E. (1921). *Language*. Harcourt Brace Jovanovich.
Sartre, J.-P. (2003). *Being and nothingness* (H. E. Barnes, Trans.; 2nd ed.). Routledge.
Schmandt-Besserat, D. (1996). *How writing came about*. University of Texas Press.
Seinfeld, J. (2020, May 6). Jerry Seinfeld: 23 hours to kill (2020)—transcript. Scraps from the loft. https://scrapsfromtheloft.com/comedy/jerry-seinfeld-23-hours-to-kill-transcript/
Shannon, C.E. & Weaver, W. (1949). *The mathematical theory of communication*. University of Illinois Press.
Shlain, L. (1991). *Art and physics*. Morrow.
Small, G., & Vorgan, G. (2008). *iBrain*. Harper.

Steinberg, S. H. (1996). *Five hundred years of printing* (rev. ed., J. Trevitt). Oak Knoll Press.
Strate, L. (1999). The varieties of cyberspace: Problems in definition and delimitation. *Western Journal of Communication 63*(3), 382–412.
Strate, L. (2003). Neil Postman, Defender of the word. *ETC.: A Review of General Semantics 60*(4), 341–350.
Strate, L. (2006). *Echoes and reflections: On media ecology as a field of study*. Hampton Press.
Strate, L. (2011a). Eine steine nacht muzak. *KronoScope 10*(1–2), 119–136.
Strate, L. (2011b). *On the binding biases of time and other essays on general semantics and media ecology*. Institute of General Semantics.
Strate, L. (2014). *Amazing ourselves to death: Neil Postman's brave new world revisited*. Peter Lang.
Strate, L. (2015). *Thunder at Darwin Station*. NeoPoiesis Press.
Strate, L. (2017a). The effects that give cause and the pattern that directs. In C. Anton, R.K. Logan, & L. Strate (Eds.), *Taking up McLuhan's cause: Perspectives on formal causality and media ecology* (pp. 93–121). Intellect.
Strate, L. (2017b). *Media ecology: An approach to understanding the human condition*. Peter Lang.
Strate, L. (2020). *Diatribal writes of passage in a world of wintertextuality: Poems on language, media, and life (but not as we know it)*. Institute of General Semantics.
Strate, L. (2022). *Concerning communication: Epic quests and lyric excursions within the human lifeworld*. Institute of General Semantics.
Strate, L. (2023). *First letter of my alphabet*. NeoPoiesis Press.
Tannen, D. (1990). *You just don't understand! Women and men in conversation*. Harper.
Trujillo Liñán, L. (2022). *Formal cause in Marshall McLuhan's thinking*. Institute of General Semantics.
Turkle, S. (2015). *Reclaiming conversation*. Penguin.
Twenge, J.M. (2023). *Generations*. Atria.
Waldrop, M.M. (1992). *Complexity*. Simon & Schuster.
Watzlawick, P., Bavelas, J.B., & Jackson, D.D. (1967). *Pragmatics of human communication*. Norton.
Watzlawick, P., Weakland, J.H., & Fisch, R. (1974). *Change*. Norton.
Wiener, N. (1950). *The human use of human beings*. Houghton Mifflin.
Wiener, N. (1961). *Cybernetics*. Houghton Mifflin.

Whitehead, A.N. & Russell, B. (1925–1927). *Principia mathematica* (2nd ed., 3 vols.). Cambridge England The University Press.

Whorf, B.L. (1956). *Language, thought, and reality*. MIT Press.

Wilden, A. (1980). *System and structure*. Routledge.

Wilson, R. A. (1990). *Quantum psychology*. Hilaritas Press.

Wittgenstein, L. (1961). *Tractatus logico-philosophicus* (D.F. Pears & B.F. McGuinness, Trans.). Routledge.

Wolf, M. (2007). *Proust and the squid*. Harper.

Wolfe, T. (1968). *The electric kool-aid acid test*. Picador.

Not A

Part 1

If Not A, **Then E**

Alfred Korzybski introduced general semantics in 1933 with the publication of his second book, *Science and Sanity*, which was subtitled, *An Introduction to Non-Aristotelian Systems and General Semantics*. He referred to non-aristotelian *systems* in the plural because, as he explained it, general semantics is not the only such system, it is one of many possible non-aristotelian systems. And it is important to note that Korzybski was not opposing everything that Aristotle stood for, but rather that he was specifically concerned with Aristotle's logic, with the mode of thought that it represented, and especially with the ways that others had used it over the centuries. Korzybski made it clear that Aristotle's logic was perfectly valid when understood as a special case that could be applied appropriately within narrow parameters. In this sense, he was following the example of non-newtonian physics, which incorporated newtonian physics as a special case within a much larger range of possibilities, and the same is true for non-euclidean geometry in relation to euclidean geometry.

- non-newtonian physics
- non-euclidean geometry
- non-aristotelian thought

The term *non-aristotelian* is sometimes abbreviated as non-A or null-A, or symbolized by the letter A with a line over it, $\bar{A}$.

Of course, non-A or null-A is basically a fancy way of saying *not A*. And to move for a moment from A to B, *NOT* is a term that is used as an operator in in Boolean logic, which is a non-aristotelian logic introduced by George Boole in the 19th century, and employed by Claude Shannon as he developed information theory in the 20th century. *NOT* is also a term that is used by S. I. Hayakawa in his famous definition of general semantics, that it is *the study of how not to make a damn fool of yourself*. Reconciling Hayakawa with Korzybski, we could define general semantics thusly: how NOT to make an ASS out of yoU and ME.

NOT A = NOT ASSUME

But I digress.

According to Boolean logic, *NOT A* would encompass everything in the universe that is not Aristotle's logic, which would include:

- Alfred Korzybski's general semantics
- the semiotics of Charles Sanders Peirce
- the New Criticism and Practical Criticism of I. A. Richards
- Alfred North Whitehead and Bertrand Russell's theory of logical types

- Ludwig Wittgenstein's concept of language games
- Susanne Langer's philosophy of symbolic form
- Claude Shannon's information theory
- Norbert Wiener's cybernetics
- Gregory Bateson's systems theory, and
- media ecology as formally introduced by Neil Postman

But the set of everything in the universe that is not Aristotle's logic would also include:

- socks
- penguins
- quarks
- cell phones
- New Zealand and
- everything from
- milkshakes to
- the Milky Way, including
- the proverbial kitchen sink.

In other words, the set of everything but Aristotle's logic is much too broad a category to be of much utility, and Korzybski has been criticized, by the rhetoric scholar Kenneth Burke (1945, 1950, 1966) among others, for representing his system in negative rather than positive terms. You might say, therefore, that Korzybski was begging the question of, what then? That is, if not A, then what?

> If Not A
> Then ?

In posing this question, I also note that IF-THEN statements are common features of the computer programming languages introduced in the 20th century, which are based on 19th century Boolean logic.

At this point, I would like to turn to another seminal thinker for one possible answer to this question—it may not be the only answer, but I do believe it is the *best* answer—and that scholar is Marshall McLuhan (1962, 1964). McLuhan would explain that Aristotle and the system of logic that he codified were products of a culture that had been radically transformed by the introduction of the Greek alphabet. To provide a brief and cursory summary,

1. the Alphabet introduced a mode of communication and a mode of thought based on the symbolic transformation of spoken words into visual records.
2. This encouraged the separation of the knower from the known, allowing the products of the mind to be viewed and reviewed, providing the critical distance that brings with it a measure of objectivity, and objectification.
3. Reading and writing also required a measure of isolation, encouraging new forms of individualism, a departure from the communal activity of speaking and listening.
4. Writing takes discourse out of its concrete situation in space and time, and its specific relationships between living, breathing human beings, and this decontextualization opens the door to high-level Abstractions and Abstract-thinking.
5. This also allows for an emphasis on Analysis, and the alphabet provides the model whereby utterances may be broken down to the basic units we call letters, the model that leads to the notion that all matter may be broken down into atoms, Atomism having been introduced by the pre-Socratic philosophers known as Ionian physicists.

6. And the alphabet brings with it a perspective that is l-i-n-e-a-r And s-e-q-u-e-n-t-i-a-l, the basis of a logic that allows for identity relationships, i.e., A=A, and transitive properties, i.e., if A=B and B=C, then A=C, as well as the Additive identity property, i.e., A+A=B, B-A=A, A+B=B+A, etc. (Carpenter, 1973; Goody, 1977; Havelock, 1963, 1982, 1986; Logan, 2004; McLuhan, 1962, 1964; Ong, 1967, 1982; Schmandt-Besserat, 1996).
7. And as I have noted elsewhere, Aristotle's logic is the logic necessitated by the experience of writing lists and organizing them by categories, or *topics*, whose root, the Greek word τόπος (*tópos*), meaning *place*, constitutes a visual metaphor. The laws of non-contradiction and excluded middle originate as practical rules to prevent double counting when you are making lists to keep track of items (Strate, 2011).

Alphabet

- **A**bstract thinking
- **A**nalysis
- **A**tomism
- l-i-n-e-a-r **A**nd s-e-q-u-e-n-t-i-a-l
- **A**=**A A**nd **A**dditive Identity Property
- **A**ristotelian logic

So, if A is for Alphabet, what then is not A? Looking backwards, we might point to Orality, as in Walter Ong's key work, *Orality and Literacy* (1982). But what Korzybski called *non*-aristotelian based on early 20th century usage would today be better referred to as *post*-aristotelian. And since orality is associated with a mode of thought that would be *pre*-aristotelian, the answer we are looking for is not the big O.

Instead, we can understand that after tens of thousands of years of orality, followed by a few thousand years of literacy, we now occupy a new era of human history, based on the technological innovation of Electricity. Indeed, McLuhan (1962, 1964) argued that the period of over two millennia of the alphabetic culture that defined the west has come to an end, replaced by the age of the Electric circuit, Electrical technology, and the Electronic media. And given our penchant for alphabetic abbreviation, it is altogether fitting that we have been using the letter E to stand for *electronic* for some time now, for the products of computer technology such as

- E-mail
- E-commerce
- E-business
- E-banking, and the
- E-books that have caused so much *agita* in the publishing industry.

We might well add to this list a term such as E-world to represent our electronic media environment. And so, McLuhan gives us the answer to the question Korzybski posed, the answer being:

If Not A
Then E

So, if Aristotle is the face of alphabetic thought, who would best represent electric consciousness? If we wanted to stay with the ancient Greeks, the answer might well be one of those Ionian physicists, namely, Heraclitus. Heraclitus was well thought of by Korzybski, Wendell Johnson (1946), and other general semanticists for his early understanding of the concept of change and the dynamic nature of reality, summed up by his famous observation that you can never step into the same river twice (because the river is always changing, but also because we are always changing as well). In contrast to other atomists such as Thales, Anaximander, Anaximenes, and Anaxagoras, who argued that elements such as water, air, and earth constitute the fundamental building blocks of the universe, Heraclitus specifically argued that, "all things are an equal exchange for fire and fire for all things, as goods are for gold and gold for goods" (quoted in Kirk, 1954, p. 345). In contrast to water, air, and earth, fire is not a type of matter, but rather a dynamic process of transformation; moreover, electricity at this time was thought to be a form of fire, later referred to as St. **E**lmo's fire. In addition to his natural philosophy, Heraclitus also placed great emphasis on *logos*, which refers to language, logic, and reason alike. And while the name Heraclitus begins with an H, the letter H comes from the Greek letter that looks like our **H**, but actually is a vowel called **E**ta, so that his name in Greek is spelled Ἡράκλειτος, and would therefore be better transliterated as *Erikleitos*, an appropriate name for our **E**-world.

But even with this revised spelling, Heraclitus is too far removed from the Electric Age to serve as an appropriate symbol for us. And when it comes to the modern discovery of electricity and electric technologies, quite a few candidates come to mind, such as:

- Benjamin Franklin, who caught lightning in a bottle;
- Luigi Galvani, who experimented on electricity in relation to the nervous system;
- Mary Shelley, who imagined the possibilities of electricity as a life force;
- André-Marie Ampère, who discovered electronmagnetism;
- Michael Faraday, who invented the electric generator;
- Samuel Morse, who invented the electrical telegraph;
- James Clerk Maxwell, whose electromagnetic theory established the existence of electromagnetic fields;
- Heinrich Hertz, who established the existence of radio waves;
- Guglielmo Marconi, inventor of the wireless;
- J. J. Thompson, who discovered the electron; and
- Nikola Tesla, whose many inventions include alternating current.

But perhaps the individual who most powerfully symbolizes electricity in the public mind, and whose last name happens to begin appropriately enough with an E, is the wizard of Menlo Park: Thomas Alva Edison. Edison's selection also harkens back to Orality, as he was the inventor of the phonograph, but he is best remembered for the Electric light, specifically the incandescent light bulb, an innovation now facing obsolescence as we move to more efficient forms of lighting. He is also known for his *Kinetoscope*, which made motion picture projection practical. But as much as he was identified with light, he had a dark side, and was severely lacking in Ethics, so Edison is not the best choice to represent our new E-world.

At this point, I would turn back to Korzybski, and consider the individual who inspired him to develop his non-aristotelian system, the scientist most closely associated with non-newtonian physics and non-euclidean geometry: Albert Einstein. Although Einstein was not associated with Electricity per se, McLuhan (1962, 1964) did identify him with the new way of thinking characteristic of the Electric age, one in which the linear and mechanistic view of space and time associated with euclidean geometry and newtonian physics was superseded by a new emphasis on discontinuities and relativities, an emphasis that can be seen in modern art as well as in physics, a parallel that Leonard Shlain (1991) further explored in detail, based on McLuhan's original insights. Einstein, of course, was famous for, among other things, an equation, specifically, $E=MC^2$, which stands for Energy equals Mass times the square of the speed of light (C).

> **Einstein's Equation**
> $$E=MC^2$$

And what this equation drives home is a notion that was building over the course of the 19th century, paralleling the development of the scientific understanding of electricity and the evolution of electric technology: the idea that energy is the basic stuff of the universe, that everything in the universe is a form of energy, even matter. Much of this understanding begins with the study of heat, giving rise to the Laws of Thermodynamics, and this brings us back to the fire of Heraclitus. But heat, electricity, and electromagnetism, light, sound, and the atomic all are forms of energy, so we can replace Electricity with Energy as the more inclusive term for our E-world, and the starting point for the E-World model I wish to develop here. Substituting Energy for Electricity also helps us to set aside minor distinctions, such as that between cables and fiber optics, or magnetic recording and optical storage media.

ENERGY

Energy was very much at the heart of Korzybski's thinking, as he was an Engineer, and originally was concerned with what he referred to as *human engineering*, by which he did not mean to imply the engineering of human beings, but rather the application of engineering principles (i.e., scientific method) by human beings to human affairs (Korzybski, 1921, 1950). As an Engineer, Koryzbski was concerned with work, which requires power, which requires energy. And he began his development of his non-aristotelian system by introducing his taxonomy of classes of life based on their utilization of energy:

- chemistry-binding plant life being based on chemical energy,
- space-binding animal life being based on kinetic energy, and
- time-binding human life being based on a special kind of potential energy, what we might call temporal energy, that is, the ability to store, preserve, and evaluate knowledge, enabling us to build on past discoveries and make progress.

The First Law of Thermodynamics expresses what is otherwise known as the conservation of Energy, that Energy cannot be created or destroyed, it can only change in quality and form, not in quantity. The Second Law of Thermodynamics states that the Energy in a closed system will tend to lose its quality over time, moving towards a state of increasingly greater disorder, randomness, and chaos, or Entropy. Things fall apart, noise invariably interferes with communication, signals degrade, there is always something lost in transmission, or translation. No matter how much time we spend cleaning house, after a while it only gets messy again. And, as Aristotle himself would put it, all of us are mortal, we are born and gestate through a process of differentiation, and that miraculous feat of organization breaks down and disintegrates when life comes to an end. Entropy is associated with the death of the individual, and the heat death of the universe, an end state where the quality of energy has run down so much as to make life impossible, and time itself comes to an end.

ENERGY

ENTROPY

Claude Shannon defined information in relation to entropy (Shannon & Weaver, 1949), and we have come to understand that information is much like a medium situated in-between chaos and order, that entropy is not all "bad," and that absolute order would represent a frozen stasis that would be just as dead as absolute chaos (Gleick, 1987; Kauffman, 1995; Maturana & Varela, 1980, 1992; Waldrop, 1992). The phrase *on the edge of chaos* has come into use to explain the ways in which systems move from states of lesser to greater complexity, going against the grain of the Second Law of Thermodynamics. The injection of a bit of entropy, in the form of random mutation, for example, or the roll of the genetic dice known as sexual reproduction, makes possible the process of Evolution, as the second direction that Energy can lead us to.

ENERGY

ENTROPY   EVOLUTION

Evolution and Entropy are not absolute opposites, but opposing tendencies of growth and dissolution, complexity and chaos. Between the two, we might look for a measure of balance, of homeostasis, that is, a dynamic state in which changes within the system allows the system to maintain itself in a seemingly unchanging fashion. In short, between Entropy and Evolution lies Equilibrium. So, having established that Energy is the starting point for our E-world, we can add that it can move in these three directions, Entropy, Evolution, and Equilibrium.

ENERGY

ENTROPY   EQUILIBRIUM   EVOLUTION

The three directions of Energy all involve the dimension of time, Entropy being identified with what has come to be known as the arrow of time, Evolution with an historical outlook, and Equilibrium with change and adjustment to meet the challenges of a dynamic environment. Einstein's non-newtonian shift from matter to energy also involved a shift from a physics that viewed the universe in absolute terms of a timeless space and a spaceless time, to a relativistic physics in which all phenomena are Events in spacetime (or more appropriate, in my view, in timespace). For this reason, I have placed Events at the center of E-world. The dimension of time is missing from Euclidean geometry and Newtonian physics, and from Aristotelian logic as well. Factoring time into the equation was a process that occurred in many different ways, from the calculus of Gottfried Leibniz and Isaac Newton to the cubism of Pablo Picasso. It includes the historical consciousness that began to emerge in the 18th century, and the theory of natural selection introduced in the 19th century by Alfred Russel Wallace and Charles Darwin. It includes Korzybski's notion of time-binding, and general semantics as a method of overcoming the fact that we tend to rely on static maps of constantly shifting territories. It includes the linguistic relativism of Edward Sapir, Dorothy Lee, and Benjamin Lee Whorf, notably Whorf's argument that Hopi and Navajo languages, with their emphasis on verbs as opposed to nouns, represent a metaphysics consonant with Einstein's non-newtonian physics. Inspired by this, Buckminster Fuller described himself by saying, *I seem to be a verb* (Fuller 1970; see also Fuller, 1963), and the scholar of Kabbalah, Rabbi David A. Cooper (1997) elaborated on the idea that God is a verb. And it includes the shift away from the visualism that dominated western culture for most of the modern era, that has its roots in ancient Greece and Rome, and towards a renewed emphasis on sound, acoustic space, and secondary orality; this shift, as discussed by McLuhan (1962, 1964) and Ong (1967, 1969, 1982), is associated with the introduction of electricity, electrical technologies, and the electronic media.

ENERGY

ENTROPY   EQUILIBRIUM   EVOLUTION

EVENTS

Media ecology, being time-oriented, has been associated with the study of Effects, especially the effects that innovations have on societies and individuals, and generally with the effects resulting from changes made to systems. And while media ecology represents an intellectual tradition and field of scholarship, McLuhan (2003) made the point that more broadly, in the age of electronic media, all of us, as a society, suddenly become concerned with the effects of things, their consequences, and not just the things themselves, as for example we become aware of and aversive to the multiple risks to health and safety that surround us (see also Perkinson 1996; Strate, 2017b). The idea of Effects tends to emphasize change over time in terms of a linear, mechanistic sequence of cause-and-effect, although in this instance Aristotle offers an alternative in which that kind of causality, known as efficient cause, is just one of four types of causation, the others being material cause, formal cause, and efficient cause (see Aristotle, 1998; Anton, Logan, & Strate, 2017; McLuhan & McLuhan, 2011; Strate, 2022; Trujillo Liñán, 2022). Formal cause in particular has been characterized as non-linear, even to the extent of allowing for effects to precede their cause (McLuhan & McLuhan, 2011). A similar view comes from systems theory and the theories of chaos and complexity, in the concept of Emergence. Rather than cause-and-effect, we have the downward causality in which new phenomena emerge out of systems as a consequence of the relationship and interaction of the parts that make up the system—the system sets the stage, opens the door to possibilities, but does not determine the outcome (Deacon, 2012). Systems themselves sometimes emerge out of the relationship and interaction of their parts, forming spontaneously, in a process called autopoiesis (Maturana & Varela, 1980, 1992). In sum, Emergence and Effects are both types of Events, resulting from the tendency of Energy to move in the direction of Entropy, or Evolution, or Equilibrium.

At this point, I think it is necessary to incorporate human subjectivity into my E-world model, as we move down from Events, to again split into three directions. The first is Experience, which represents the individual's relationship to reality.

ENERGY

ENTROPY   EQUILIBRIUM   EVOLUTION

EVENTS

EXPERIENCE

The relationship between Events and Experience corresponds to broadly to Korzybski's (1933/2023) model of the process of abstracting, which he referred to as the Structural Differential.

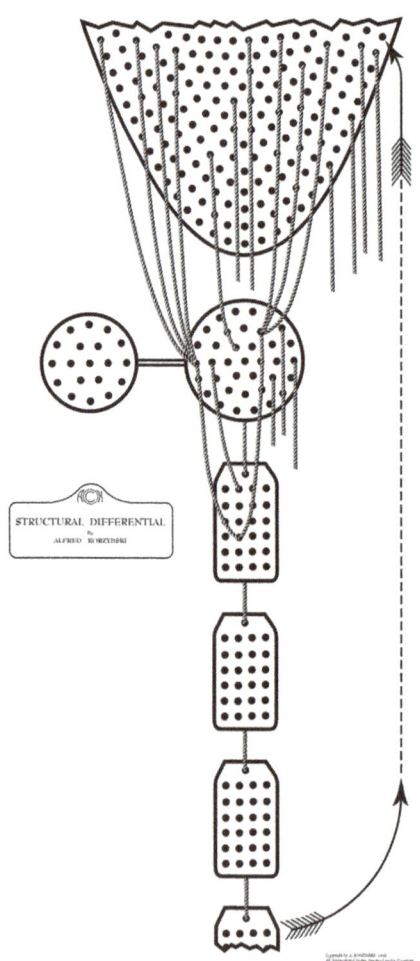

At the top of that model is the Event Level, depicted as a broken parabola, representing objective reality, which is to say Einstein's events in spacetime, and this corresponds to Events in the E-world model. In the structural differential, the strings represent the process of Abstracting, and the circle represents the Object Level, which corresponds to non-verbal perception, the basis of Experience in the E-world model. For human beings, the process of abstracting continues with the addition of language, and moves to higher order abstractions as we move from the specific to the general, from naming and describing to inferring and generalizing, leaving out more and more details and becoming increasingly more subjective in our Evaluations. Experience then includes the entirety of the structural differential apart from the event level.

Experience is a subjective phenomenon, but subjectively, we tend to relate to Events as Objects, and this opens the door for the concept of Objectivity, and a tendency towards Objectification. We are in the habit of relating to phenomena as *things*, and general semantics represents an attempt to put us closer in touch with the world as Events in spacetime (Hayakawa & Hayakawa, 1990; Johnson, 1946; Korzybski, 1933/2023; see also Ong, 1969). But the experience of objects or things does not constitute the entirety of human engagement with the world, and so we have to look elsewhere for the other elements on this level. Experience here corresponds to what Martin Buber (1970) referred to as I-It relationships, but what of the I-Thou, or I-You relations, our relationship to other human beings, insofar as we regard them as fellow persons and not things? I have represented that element by the term Empathy, because that is what language and symbolic communication unlock in us, the ability to feel for others, imagine what it is like to experience the world as others, and see ourselves as others see us. And the ability to employ theory of mind, that is, the theory that others have a mind, a consciousness, much like our own (Baron-Cohen, 1995; Frith, 1989; see also Strate, 2022).

To understand Empathy, we have to draw upon the symbolic interactionist perspective of George Herbert Mead (1934), Hugh Duncan (1962, 1968), and Erving Goffman (1959), the humanist psychotherapy of Carl Rogers (1951) and Abraham Maslow (1954), and the relational approach of Gregory Bateson (1972, 1979), Paul Watzlawick (Watzlawick, Bavelas, & Jackson, 1967; Watzlawick, Weakland, & Fisch, 1974), and Deborah Tannen (1990).

ENERGY

ENTROPY   EQUILIBRIUM   EVOLUTION

EVENTS

EXPERIENCE   EMPATHY

As we move from the monologic of Experience to the dialogic of Empathy, the next step over is to the eco-logic of Ecology. I use Ecology here to represent the complexities of interactions among many different people that make up our social lives. Ecology represents our social networks, both face-to-face and technologically mediated, including family and friends, neighbors and communities, professional affiliations and amateur associations, and societies and cultures. And to understand Ecology, we need to turn to the work of scholars such as Lewis Mumford (1934, 1952, 1961, 1967, 1970), Harold Innis (1951, 1972), Eric Havelock (1963, 1978, 1982, 1986), Jacques Ellul (1964, 1965, 1980, 1985, 1990), Elizabeth Eisenstein (1979), Jack Goody (1977), and Denise Schmandt-Besserat (1996). And of course, McLuhan (1962, 1964, 2003; McLuhan & Fiore, 1967; McLuhan & McLuhan, 2011), Ong (1967, 1982), and Postman (1970, 1974, 1976, 1985, 1992, 1995; Postman & Weingartner, 1969).

ENERGY

ENTROPY   EQUILIBRIUM   EVOLUTION

EVENTS

EXPERIENCE   EMPATHY   ECOLOGY

Experience, Empathy, and Ecology are not isolated elements, but rather interact with one another in myriad ways, so that, for example, our relationships influence the way that we experience the world and abstract our reality. These three forms of human engagement with Events correspond to three main types of communication, the intrapersonal, the interpersonal, and the group. And they correspond to the most basic concept of numbering, one, two, and many.

The three aspects of human subjectivity converge once again, so that Experience, Empathy, and Ecology together constitute our relationship to our Environment, as things and objects make up our environment, but so do others, other human beings, other conscious agents, whether encountered in a one-to-one relationship, or in a network of relations that forms a group. Korzybski (1933/2023) described his perspective as that of "the-organism-as-a-whole-in-an environment" (p. liv) and the inclusion of Environment here also reminds us to maintain a holistic perspective in regard to the different elements that make up this model, and to employ a systems orientation. And McLuhan (1964) emphasized the fact that we are actively engaged with our environments, influencing and altering them to the point of creating new human environments through our media and technologies, at the same time that we ourselves are shaped and molded by our environments (see also Strate, 2017b). Environment, then, is properly located at the base of this E-world model.

ENERGY

ENTROPY   EQUILIBRIUM   EVOLUTION

EVENTS

EXPERIENCE   EMPATHY   ECOLOGY

ENVIRONMENT

The nine elements identified so far have been arranged in a hierarchical fashion, but I want to emphasize that they are all connected to one another, all interconnected to form a complete system. And, underlying all of these elements, as the foundation of the model, is the simple fact of Existence.

This connects the E-world model to the philosophical movement of Existentialism associated with Jean-Paul Sartre (2003), Simone de Beauvoir (2015), and Maurice Merlau-Ponty (1962). And to draw on general semantics once more, Existence also covers what we might just call Et cetera, by which we mean, *and Everything Else*. For this reason, Existence needs to be located at the foundation of the E-world model.

ENERGY

ENTROPY EQUILIBRIUM EVOLUTION

EVENTS

EXPERIENCE EMPATHY ECOLOGY

ENVIRONMENT

EXISTENCE

While this may seem to complete the model, I think it important to acknowledge the possibility of something beyond the material world we inhabit, and to make the model relevant for those of you of a spiritual bent. With this in mind, I would crown the model on top with Elohim, which is the Hebrew word for God. This covers the monotheistic religions, and as for any pagans, neo-paganists, animists, and the like who might object, although Elohim is translated as God, grammatically it is a plural noun, and therefore covers polytheism as well. Some students of Kabbalah embrace a less personal concept of the divine or supernatural, an understanding of Elohim as the Ein Sof, the infinite, which is consonant with forms of eastern mysticism, as well as the basic notion of the sacred, as in the concept of sacred time and space discussed by Mircea Eliade (1954, 1959). Elohim can also serve as a metaphor for the transcendental quality of nature, as it did for Baruch Spinoza. And it can simply stand in for our sense of awe at the wonders of the universe, for the mysteries of life and death that we may never solve. In the words of Albert Einstein:

> The most beautiful thing we can experience is the mysterious. It is the source of all true art and all science. He to whom this emotion is a stranger, who can no longer pause to wonder and stand rapt in awe, is as good as dead: his eyes are closed. The insight into the mystery of life, coupled though it be with fear, has also given rise to religion. To know what is impenetrable to us really exists, manifesting itself as the highest wisdom and the most radiant beauty, which our dull faculties can comprehend only in their most primitive forms—this knowledge, this feeling is at the center of true religiousness. (Einstein, Dewey, Jeans, Wells, Dreiser, Mencken, Adams, Peterkin, Keith, Babbit, Webb, Krutch, Nansen, Mumford, Millikan, Shih, Belloc, Haldane, Nathan, Edman, Russell, & Ralphinge, 1931, p. 6)

With this in mind, I believe I can proceed with Einstein's tacit blessing to include Elohim as the final element that completes the E-world model.

ELOHIM

ENERGY

ENTROPY   EQUILIBRIUM   EVOLUTION

EVENTS

EXPERIENCE   EMPATHY   ECOLOGY

ENVIRONMENT

EXISTENCE

At this point, I think it also significant to note that, taken as whole, this model for E-world resembles the Tree of Life diagram of the Kabbalah.

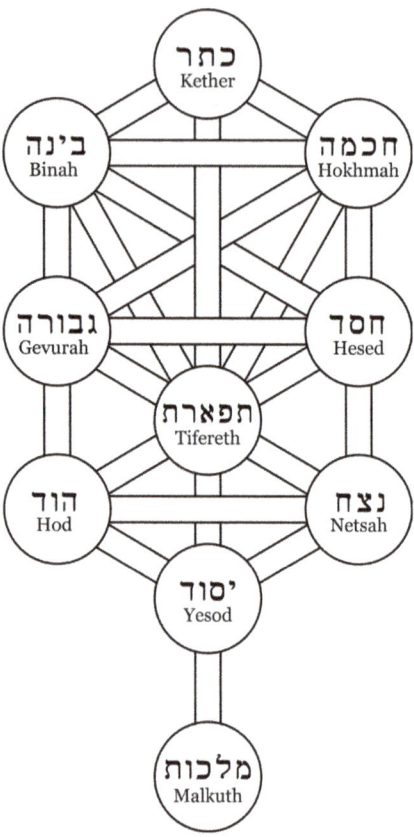

I certainly did not set out to construct a model on that basis. My original intent was to follow Korzybski's (1933/2023) example in pursuing a form of consilience by bringing together our scientific understanding of the universe with our philosophical understanding of what Hannah Arendt refers to as the human condition (Arendt, 1958), as informed by the work of media ecology scholars such as McLuhan (1962, 1964) and Postman (1976, 1985, 1992, 1995), and of course my own thoughts on the subject (see, for example, Strate 2011, 2017b, 2022). But as I was developing the model, it quite naturally fell into that archetype. So perhaps, in place of the Kabbalistic Tree of Life, this represents the E of Life.

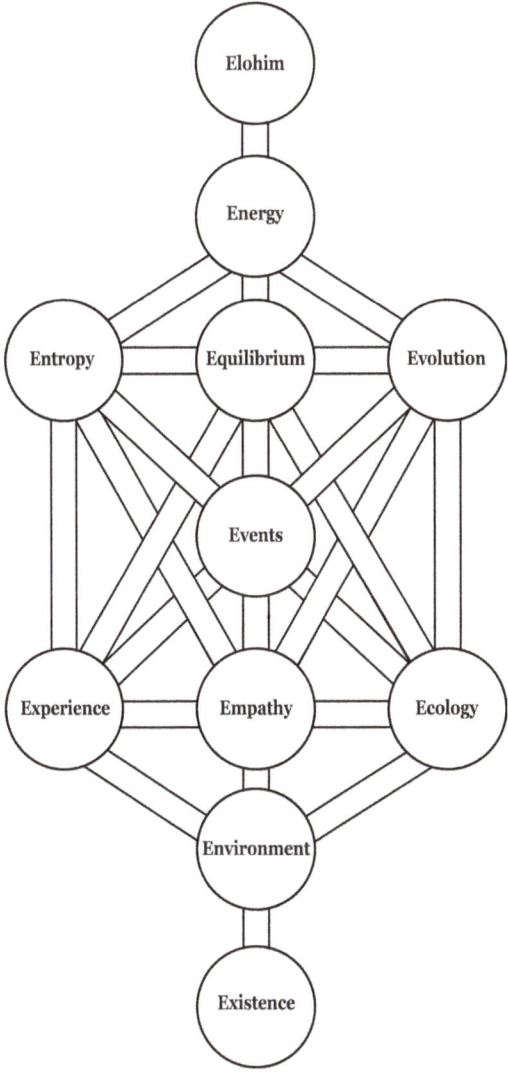

One difference, however, is that the Tree of Life has ten elements, or Sephirot, which represent ten aspects of the Divine, the ten media, if you will, of the Ein Sof, the infinite. The E of Life, however, does not stop at ten parts, but instead goes up to Eleven. And that may be a difference that does not make a difference, but even so, there is a way to solve the incongruity. Again, using the Kabbalah as inspiration, we can consider Existence and Elohim as two aspects of the same element, not two separate elements, and in doing so connect the top of the model to the bottom of the model in circular fashion. This is only fitting for E-World, given that Electricity requires a circuit, Einstein's non-newtonian physics established that space is curved, and even Aristotle knew that the world is round.

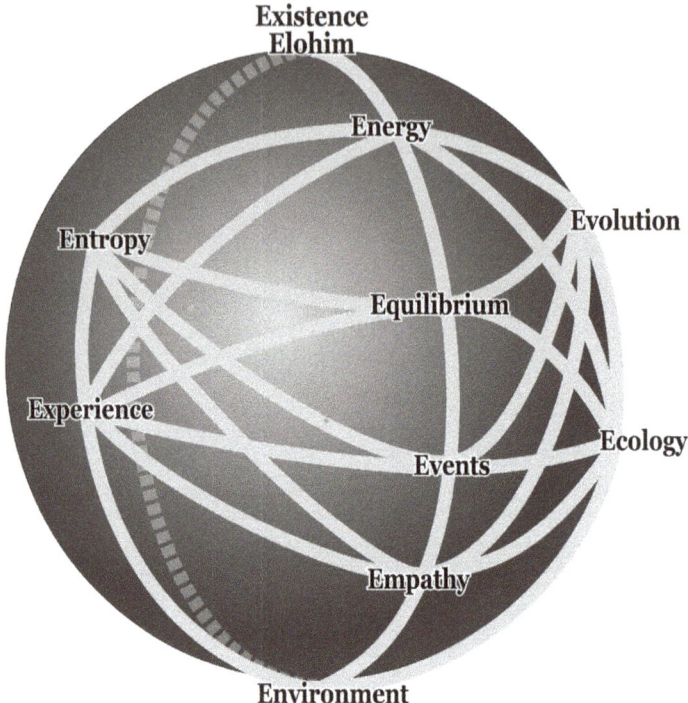

The original Tree of Life of legend was said to exist in the Garden of Eden. As you may recall, there was a bit of a snafu back in Eden concerning Eve, and involving an Apple, which brings us back to the beginning, not just Genesis, but back to A. The Apple came from the Tree of Knowledge, not the Tree of Life, and the A of Alphabet and the A of Aristotle's logic represents innovations of the greatest importance in our ability to obtain and maintain knowledge. Having eaten of the Apple, and gained that knowledge, it is now time for us to move on to the next stage, which is not a return to the past, not a step back to Eden as a golden Age, nor a step up to Eden as the Afterlife. Rather, it is time for the creation of a new Eden, right here, right now, on our one and only E-World, Planet Earth.

E-World

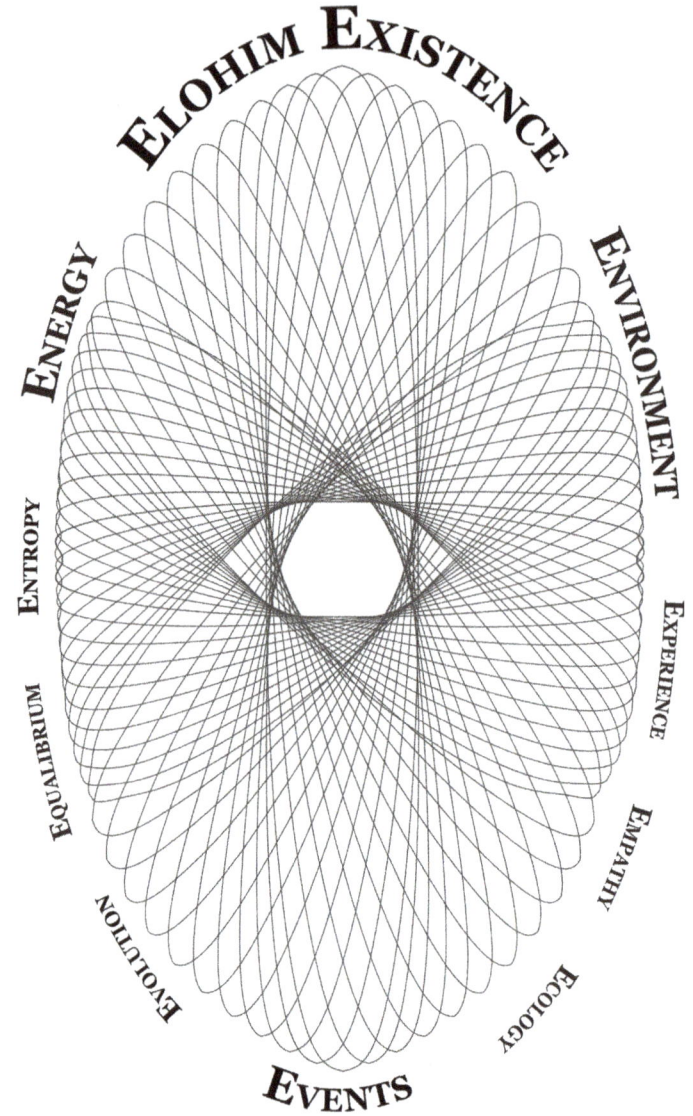

If Not A Then E

Word, Image, **Number**

I

A picture is worth a thousand words. It's a familiar saying, but what does it really mean? Taken literally, it suggests something along the lines of a mathematical equation:

$$\text{PICTURE} = \text{WORD} \times 1{,}000$$

And if you remember your arithmetic, it would also imply the following:

$$\text{WORD} = \text{PICTURE} \div 1{,}000$$

But does this formula really add up? Can words and pictures be reduced to quantities to be plugged into two sides of an equals sign? Or are numbers something altogether different from both words and images?

Numbers represent *quantities*. The difference between two different numbers is a quantitative difference.

Images deal with *qualities*, specifically qualities relating to visual appearance, to perception. The difference between two different images is a qualitative difference.

Words deal with *qualities* as well, and the difference between two different words is also a qualitative difference (except in a sense for words that stand for numbers, which I will account for in section IV).

But the qualities that words deal with are conceptual rather than perceptual, relating to thought rather than sensation.

In other words, the qualities that words deal with are different from the qualities that images deal with. The difference between words and pictures is not a quantitative difference. It is a qualitative difference.

Or to return again to mathematical notation, the first two equations are wrong, and instead the reality is more like this:

$$PICTURE \neq WORD$$

$$WORD \neq NUMBER$$

$$PICTURE \neq NUMBER$$

Or to invoke a different saying, what we are dealing with here are apples and oranges (and bananas, if we count numbers as well)!

Simply put, pictures, words, and numbers represent different *codes*, different modes of communication, different types of symbolic form, different types of *signs* that in turn are associated with different modes of *sign*ification. As Alfred Korzybski (1933/2023) make clear in his introduction to general semantics, they are different ways of *abstracting* information out of our environment, as we can only take in a part of the unknowable whole that is out there. And they are different ways of *mapping* or otherwise *representing* reality, or at least our perceptions and conceptions about our external environment, and about our own internal world of thoughts and feelings.

Pictures, words, numbers, and other forms such as gesture, dance, and music, are the tools we use to make sense out of our world, to make meaning out of our experience, to create—in the sense that our understanding of reality is a social and psychological construct—a reality that we can live within. They are the tools our minds use to help us to know our world, to create an illusion of order and stability out of the chaos and unpredictability of the outer environment, and to find ways to act upon and alter our environment, with the goal of making it more conducive to our own survival.

Pictures, words, numbers, etc., are tools, but they are different tools, in the same way that hammers, scissors, and screwdrivers are different tools, used to perform different tasks, best suited for certain tasks and able to perform others only with difficulty at best, and often not at all. Put another way, each tool has its own particular *bias*.

As tools, pictures, words, numbers, etc., are different from one another, qualitatively different from one another, and these differences are *differences that make a difference*, to use Gregory Bateson's (1972) famous phrase. And because they are differences that make a difference, it follows that *the medium is the message*, as Marshall McLuhan (1964) so aptly put it.

Of course, the question then is, what is the difference between the word and the image?

II

Pictures and words are like apples and oranges, different in kind. They are different forms of representation, different tools for thinking about the world. To play off of a popular book title, words are from Mars, and pictures are from Venus.

So when people say that *a picture is worth a thousand words*, all that really means is that pictures are better at certain tasks than words. What the popular saying leaves out is the fact that words are better than pictures at other tasks. But let's start with what pictures do particularly well, with the *bias* of the image as a symbolic form, as a medium.

Consider this: What's the least interesting part of any novel? I think you may agree that it's the passages that describe scenery or, really, any kind of detailed description. All they do is interrupt the narrative flow, putting the plotline on pause.

When a filmmaker decides to turn a novel into a motion picture, the adaptation will pick up on key actions and events that take place in the story, and the important dialogue spoken by the characters. The novel's descriptive passages, on the other hand, will be left to the set designers and cinematographers, to be conveyed by images rather than words.

If the goal is to convey an accurate sense of what something looks like, words fall short. All they can do is de-*scribe*, in a sense, to circum-*scribe*, to circle around the subject rather than getting directly to the point. When it comes to appearances, it is much more effective to show than to tell—you might say it's a thousand times better (but only if you mean it figuratively, not literally).

On the other hand, have you ever gone to see a movie that was based on a novel that you dearly loved, only to be disappointed with the adaptation? If so, you're not alone, in fact, it's a pretty common experience. Adaptations rarely meet our expectations, unless of course the original was not very good to begin with, or something we didn't really care for. The reason for the let down has much to do with the disconnect between what we imagined in our mind's eye, and what we see on the screen.

The ambiguity of words, when it comes to verbal description, has its advantages. Words require us to use our imagination, to *visualize* for ourselves what places, persons, and things look like. And as McLuhan (1964) explains, when we don't get all of the information, when we're forced to fill in what's missing, we are much more actively participating in creating the message than we otherwise would be. We're involved, we're invested, we're co-creators.

But when the image is just handed to us wholesale, we don't have to work quite so hard to get the message, to make sense out of it, and that has real advantages beyond the accuracy of the depiction, simply because it requires less energy, or if you like, less mental processing power from us. But at the same time the message is less a part of us, we're less committed and connected to it. It simply doesn't matter as much to us, it's less significant, less meaningful.

When we're involved and participating, when words trigger visualization, each person's imagination can take that individual somewhere altogether different and distinct from anyone else's. This presents a problem if we're talking about the real world, but after all it's not so terrible a problem for fiction, and in fact can be a real advantage in enhancing its appeal.

And when we've already built up our own ideas about what things and people and places look like, and then are shown images that will invariably vary from our own imaginations, the result can easily be deeply disappointing. This comes up not just for film adaptations, but also in making music videos—in fact, it was a common complaint back when music videos first became a popular phenomenon, soon after MTV was launched on August 1st, 1981.

The difference between verbal imagination and visual depiction was also very much a part of the transition between radio to television in the postwar era. And the difference between the ability to communicate mainly through words on radio and the ability to transmit pictures through television was of extraordinary significance.

III

For the generation raised on radio, as depicted in Woody Allen's 1987 film *Radio Days*, one of the things they loved about the medium was the fact that it evoked, appealed to, and required the use of the imagination. When television was introduced, some lamented the loss of this quality, as television's ability to show us things overshadowed radio's emphasis on the use of the human voice to tell us about them. There was something personal about the microphone, something somehow cold, distanced, and dehumanized about the camera.

Something similar happened when MTV first appeared in 1981. The first music video played on the new cable channel minutes after they began operations was, appropriately enough, "Video Killed the Radio Star" by The Buggles. At that time, the music video format was all but unknown, but it quickly became a popular culture phenomenon. And not surprisingly, many people criticized this development, pointing out that what they loved about popular music was the fact that they could use their imaginations to visualize what the song was about, and that adding video to the music short-circuited this process. Of course, others saw the music video as a new art form.

The contrast between audio and audiovisual media also becomes apparent every year at the Oscars, when they give the award for sound effects, and show film clips without any sound at all, and then again with the sound. That comparison brings home the fact that the soundtrack has much to do with the impact of what we see on the screen. Sound is visceral, hitting us in the gut, while visuals keep us at a distance, as observers, as spectators, as voyeurs.

And to return to the difference between radio and television, it is worth noting that both are electronic media, both able to transmit messages instantaneously, to present aspects of the world *live*, and both are forms of broadcasting, meaning that they could get those live messages out to massive audiences simultaneously. But what makes the social, cultural, and psychological impact of television so much more extensive, dramatic, and explosive, in contrast to radio, is exactly its ability to show instead of just tell.

Walter Ong (1967) uses the example of a sports broadcast to drive home this point. Listen to a game on radio, and we are completely dependent on the announcers to paint a verbal picture, to provide us with a *report* on what is going on. No matter how quickly they get their message out to us, the report is still about something that just happened. They may use the present tense, but what they are describing has already occurred, so that in effect the message is conveyed in the past tense.

In this sense, radio reports are not different in kind from reports in newspapers, they're just conveyed faster, that's all. It's as if there's a barrier between a sense of the past and a sense of the present that cannot be overcome by words alone. But that particular time barrier can be broken by pictures.

Watch a game on television, and the result is completely different from listening to it on radio. We see the action as it's happening, in the present tense. The announcers are still lagging behind the action, responding to it, and reporting on it. And arguably, whatever they're saying is entirely unnecessary, as we can see what is going on for ourselves. There even have been some experiments with televising games without any announcers. And while their commentary may add something appealing, worthwhile, maybe even valuable to the viewers' experience, the audience is no longer dependent on reports, or the individuals providing them to us.

The difference between showing and telling is the difference between the present and the past, between intimacy and distance, and between accuracy and imagination. Each mode has its advantages and disadvantages. But there are differences that are still more significant, differences between simple percepts and more elusive concepts. But this one set of contrasts can help us to begin to think about the many other differences that can be studied through a media ecology approach, the many other differences that make a difference.

IV

Before continuing to discuss the difference between images and words, let's pause to consider the difference between images and numbers once again. It is true that images can be digitized, reduced to a series of zeroes and ones in binary code. But the numbers do not add up to the equivalent of what the image depicts. Simply put:

000111111011000000000 ≠ 🙂

The sequence of zeroes and ones, or electrical impulses, do not convey the same meaning as the image. The binary code may signify a series of yes or no messages, or on or off signals. They may provide instructions on how to produce the image on a screen or on paper. But they do not represent the same *thing* or *concept* or *feeling* as the icon does. In other words:

NUMBER ≠ IMAGE

Numbers are abstract whereas images are concrete. You can isolate the number 2, remove it from any specific context, consider it on its own as a pure concept, a *twoness*. But if you want to illustrate the number two with pictures, you have to show two pictures of *something*, 2 pictures of the sun, 2 pictures of a cat, two pictures of a glass of water. It follows that:

2 ≠ 🙂🙂

It also follows that 2 apples are not the same as 2 oranges. For that matter, one pair of apples would not be exactly the same as another pair of apples, even though they would represent the same *number* of apples. There will always be qualitative differences between any two pairs of apples, or between any two apples by themselves, or even between any one apple over time as it is subject to constant change. We could even recognize that:

Even though the images of either side of the equation appear to be identical, there will always be minute differences between two, at the very least due to the ongoing dynamic dance of particles and energy on the subatomic level.

On the other hand, we all learn at an early age about equations such as:

$$1 + 1 = 2$$

Which also implies the truism that:

$$2 = 2$$

Numbers represent abstract quantities. Images represent concrete qualities. Numbers therefore are rational, literally so given that the root meaning of *rationality* is *ratio*. Images on the other hand are emotional; they convey or elicit feelings.

Like images, words can be digitized. The word *apple* translated into binary code would be *01100001 01110000 01110000 01101100 01100101*. But once again, the series of zeroes and ones do not convey the same meaning as the words. In this regard, we can say that:

$$WORD \neq NUMBER$$

Like images, words can represent qualities. But not the same kinds of qualities as images. As previously noted, words are conceptual whereas images are perceptual, so that whatever images can show us, words can only tell us about. Words can only provide us with a relatively vague idea of what images can convey. At best, the words *smiley face* could only provide an approximate equivalent of a picture of smiley face:

$$smiley\ face \cong \text{☺}$$

Words therefore are more abstract than images, even when words provide a concrete description. In fact, while words can represent qualities, they can also represent quantities. The word *two* represents a specific quantity, whether the word is said out loud, written out, or expressed by the numeral *2*. In this sense, while words are not numbers, numbers can in fact be conveyed via words:

$$\text{NUMBER} = \text{WORD}$$

You may note that this violates the commutative property of mathematics. But this brings to the fore the simple point that:

$$\text{LANGUAGE} \neq \text{MATHEMATICS}$$

The closest language comes to mathematics is with formal logic. Frustration with the limitations of language led to the invention of symbolic logic, where words are largely replaced by symbolic notation similar to that of mathematics. Frustration with the limitations of logic, in turn, led to the invention of general semantics, where deduction takes a back seat to induction and empiricism based on scientific method.

Simply put, words are not numbers but numbers can be words, numbers in one sense are a subset of words. They are a special case within the general category of linguistic expression. We can consider mathematics as a separate symbol system in its own right, but one that only exists for us because language exists. Also, within mathematics, geometry only exists for us because we have the capacity to create and interpret images.

As symbols, numbers are valued because they are precise and unambiguous. Not only can we say that:

$$2 = 2$$

But we can also say that:

$$2 \neq 3$$

And:

$$2 \neq 4$$

And for that matter

$$2 \neq 1$$
$$2 \neq 0$$
$$2 \neq \tfrac{1}{2}$$
$$2 \neq 42$$
$$2 \neq 10^{1,000,000,000,000,000}$$

As well as:

$$2 \neq \infty$$

This last equation states that two is not equal to infinity, but also can convey the fact that there are an infinite number of quantities that two is not equal to.

V

Numbers are discrete units with precise and unambiguous meanings. The symbol has a one-to-one relationship with what it represents. This is what is meant by the term *digital*. The word *digit* is a synonym for *number*. Digit also refers to fingers (and toes). The obvious connection is that when we first learn to count, we typically count on our fingers, we also learn to hold our fingers up to indicate a particular number, and we count things in our environment by pointing to or touching them. That is why McLuhan (1964) argues that numbers are an extension of the sense of touch, thereby linking our most abstract symbolic form with our most concrete form of sense perception.

Words are less precise and more ambiguous than numbers. When numbers are used to represent any aspect of the environment, they only abstract out of the environment quantities, leaving qualities behind. Words abstract both quantities and qualities, and can pick and choose between the two, and among the innumerable qualities that exist in the world.

But words are similar to numbers in that words are discrete units. And while words can have multiple definitions, they can be clearly defined, and operational definitions can be specified. Words can be collected in vocabulary lists, and their definitions compiled in dictionaries.

Words are the basic units of speech and language. In linguistics, the technical term is *morpheme*. Words are morphemes, units that are associated with meaning. And so are prefixes and suffixes. *Anti-* means against, *de-* means opposite, *inter-* means between, *re-* means again, *un-* means not, *-ed* means past tense, *-ment* means process or action, and *-s* means more than one. None of these are considered words, but they are also units that we combine in various ways in speaking or writing.

Morphemes themselves are composed of other units termed *phonemes*. A phoneme is a basic unit of sound within a given language. Every language has its own particular set of phonemes, which may not have meaning, but do make a difference in the meaning of words.

Apart from the units that make up a language, there are rules for how to combine those units. Those rules are what we commonly refer to as grammar, although in linguistics the term used is *syntax*.

Words are units made up of other units. They are associated with certain meanings, and are also combined with other words according to certain rules to generate additional meaning. These combinations include what we refer to as statements, reports, commands, and questions.

The meaning of any given word is almost always arbitrary. The spoken or written word is not similar in any way to whatever it represents. The word *face* does not look like a face. The word *fire* is no different in actual temperature from other words. The word *chocolate* does not display the color nor taste like the actual substance. That is why different languages are different. The same animal that in English we call a *cat* can be called a *gato* in Spanish, a *macska* in Hungarian, a *kissa* in Finnish, a *bilāḍī* in Gujarati, a *neko* in Japanese, a *popoki* in Hawaiian, etc. The only reason why the word *cat* means what it does is because we all were taught that that is what it means. The meaning of words are based on tacit agreement, which is to say that they are conventional.

Images are not made up of discrete units. They are continuous, irreducible wholes. You cannot take a picture apart, line by line, brush stroke by brush stroke, dot by dot, pixel by pixel, and isolate meaningful units. As Susanne Langer (1957) explains, there is no equivalent of dictionary definitions for images, and neither is there the equivalent of dictionaries themselves where you can look up the meaning of an image.

The meaning of an image is not arbitrary. It is based on resemblance. A picture of a face captures something of the appearance of a face, abstracting out of an actual face some of its characteristics. The smiley face image resembles the general shape of a head, the placement of two eyes and the upturned curve of a smile:

The definition of the smiley face image, however, is highly ambiguous. Does it represent smiling as a facial expression? Is it saying I am happy? Is it telling you to smile? Does it refer to some other statement I've made? If so, is it saying that this is a good thing? Does it mean I am joking? Does it mean I'm being ironic? Does it mean I like you? Am I mocking you? Am I simply saying hello? Or maybe goodbye? Have a nice day?

Images are not digital. The opposite of digital is *analogical*, meaning *not logical*. Their meaning is based on some type of similarity, on resemblance, on *analogy*. The grooves on a vinyl record album are an analog of the vibrations that sound makes, as opposed to the MP3 digital recording that consists of zeroes and ones. The clock face is an analog of the sun's circuit across the sky, as opposed to the numerical readout of a digital clock or watch.

Nonverbal communication is mostly analogical, the exception being emblems that take the place of words, such as using your fingers to indicate a specific number, giving a thumbs up sign, nodding or shaking your head to indicate yes or no, etc. Sense perception is largely analogical as well. Iain McGilchrist (2009) explains that, generally speaking, the characteristics associated with the left hemisphere of the brain are digital, while the right hemisphere is analogical. Most of our brain activity is analogical, most of human activity is analogical (Langer, 1957; Nystrom, 2021, 2022), most of what we truly are is analogical.

VI

Look!
Listen!
Go!
Stay!
Sit!
Stand!
Yes.
No.
Maybe …
Ok?

A single word can function on its own as a complete sentence. But for the most part, we put one word after another just as we put one foot after another when we're walking. Or like putting one bead after another on a string to form a necklace or bracelet. Or when we attach one link to another to form a chain.

Words typically are not hermits or lone wolves. They're social creatures. They crave the company of others like themselves.

In other words, language is sequential. It's like history, *one damn thing after another*, except that what you are reading is one damn word after another, made up of one damn letter after another, displayed on one damn line after another, appearing on one damn page after another, structured by one damn sentence after another, making up one damn paragraph after another, in turn making up one damn chapter after another, etc.

When we're speaking, it's one damn sound after another, the sequence existing in time rather than displayed in space. It's one damn syllable after another, one damn utterance after another, and still, one damn word after another.

Words as discrete units combine to form sentences that function as certain kinds of statements.

One type of statement is a definition. According to Merriam-Webster, the word cat is defined as "a carnivorous mammal (*Felis catus*) long domesticated as a pet and for catching rats and mice" or "any of a family (*Felidae*) of carnivorous usually solitary and nocturnal mammals (such as the domestic cat, lion, tiger, leopard, jaguar, cougar, wildcat, lynx, and cheetah)," along with several other meanings.

Definitions are statements that use words to define other words. Those words are also defined by other words. We can define the verb *can* as meaning *able*, and we can then define the word *able* as meaning *can*. Definitions will eventually lead us in circles. They are tautologies (Condon, 1985). And dictionaries are closed systems, which is why a foreign language dictionary is not very helpful if you don't already know the language.

Statements of definitions use words to define words, but we can also use illustrations to supplement or even replace definitions, as in:

smiley face = 🙂

And we can also use words to define an image, as in:

🙂 = smiley face

But, while we can use words to define other words, we cannot create the equivalent of a statement of definition through images alone:

 = ?

What image would you place on the other side of the above equation? I can define the words *smiley face* as *an icon that resembles the human facial expression of smiling*, but what kind of image could you show that would explain what a smiley face represents? The answer is that images alone cannot convey definitions.

Another type of statement is one that expresses a judgment or opinion. I can say that the sunset is beautiful, and I could produce a painting of a sunset that a viewer might say is beautiful, but there is no way to indicate through images the statement that *the painting is beautiful*, or for that matter the statement that *the sunset itself is beautiful*. I can say that slavery is evil, and I can display an image showing slaves being mistreated, but I cannot actually identify the individuals as slaves, as opposed to prisoners for example, or express the general notion of evil except by specific actions. I cannot depict the concept of slavery itself, or the value judgment that the entire institution of slavery is itself evil, as opposed to, say, the idea that mistreatment of slaves is unfortunate. I can express an opinion about the issue of abortion, and again I can produce images that support that position in some way or express some of the feelings that accompany it, but I cannot produce the equivalent of a statement of opinion through images alone.

I can issue a command, such as, *bring me a cup of coffee*. I cannot issue an order simply by drawing a picture, unless the context has already been established through words. Otherwise, the meaning of the image is not clear. Am I merely showing off my artistic skills, expressing a general preference, depicting a beverage I consumed in the past, offering the other person a cup, or wanting some other beverage? Is it a command, making a request, asking for a favor? Images alone cannot take the place of a command.

I can ask a question, such as, *how are you? Are you feeling all right?* But how do I ask a question through images alone? Images do not interrogate.

I can make a claim, such as, it is *raining outside right now*. That claim can be verified by you, assuming there is a window or door nearby. In this way, a statement can be determined true or false. Images, however, do not make claims, and therefore cannot be proven true or false. If I show you an image of rain, even an image of rain falling outside of wherever we are, there is no claim being made unless I use my words and say, *this is what is happening outside right now*. And even then, it would be the verbal statement that is true of false, not the picture.

In this sense, images are not statements. They do not make arguments. They can be used as evidence to support a claim, but they make no claim unless we add words to them. Digital codes like language and numbers can make statements that can be evaluated. These types of codes are also referred to as *discursive*, and when they are used to make claims that can be evaluated as true or false, they are *propositional* in form. Langer (1957) refers to analogical codes as *presentational*, because they *present* us with concrete experiences, rather than make statements of any kind.

Images can be manipulated. Images can be faked. But even a counterfeit is not false in and of itself. What is false is any claim that it is genuine, which requires a statement made through language (Carpenter, 1973). What is false is any attribution given to it, which has to be made through words. The image by itself makes no claim as to its authenticity, its provenance, or what it represents.

Images, being neither true nor false, and being ambiguous in their meaning, require interpretation. That is what we look for when we go to an art museum, look at a painting, and then look at the sign to read the name of the artist and the title of the work. We hope thereby to get some indication of what the painting is supposed to depict or represent. Of course, viewers are perfectly free to interpret the work in their own way, and this is true of all art forms, including literary works that are created with words. But only words can be used to form scientific theories and hypotheses that can be tested, such as *the earth revolves around the sun*.

Images, being neither true nor false, and being ambiguous in meaning, can be used in different ways. The same image can be taken out of its original context and used over and over again to support different claims. The image of a young child bleeding from a playground accident can be used by propagandists as evidence of harm inflicted by a military attack, and can be used repeatedly in response to different conflicts over time. The image of a bombed out building can be used by one side to illustrate how the enemy destroyed a civilian residence, and by the other side how their air force destroyed a munitions factory (and both claims could be true at the same time!).

Images are irrational. They evoke feelings and emotions, and elicit a visceral response. Numbers are rational and distancing. A quantitative orientation is cold and calculating. Stalin famously said that *a single death is a tragedy, a millions deaths is a statistic*. Words can do both. They represent balance between the two extremes.

Over the past two centuries, we have come to be dominated more and more by images, through the invention of photography, the development of various technologies for the mechanical reproduction of art, the motion picture, television, and the proliferation of digital technologies and screens. Our public discourse has become increasingly more irrational as a result (Boorstin, 1978; Postman, 1985; Strate, 2011b, 2014).

Over the past two centuries, we have come to be dominated more and more by technical procedures and devices based on numbers and quantification, from industrialism, scientific management, Fordism, information technology, statistical analysis, computers and digital devices, and our institutions have become increasingly more hyper-rational as a result (Beniger, 1986; Perkinson, 1996; Postman, 1992; Strate, 2011b, 2014).

What is missing is the sense of balance we once achieved among the spoken, written, and printed word, the media environment that gave birth to the Enlightenment, modern science, and modern democracy.

That sense of balance is what Postman (1999) wanted us to retrieve as we prepared to enter the 21st century, and that we still need to retrieve nearly a quarter of the way in.

The only hope we have to regain balance is to restore the word to its rightful place, as the happy medium between image and number, and as our primary mode of expression, cognition, and communication.

Not Be

Part 2

It Is What **It Isn't**

In the Preface to his book entitled *Conscientious Objections*, Neil Postman (1988) writes that "grievance is the source of all interesting prose" (p. xi). Whether or not my commentary is at all interesting I will leave up to you. But I can affirm that it begins with a grievance. Or maybe it is more of a pet peeve, a minor annoyance rather than the sort of thing that could spark a protest movement. But in any case, I hope to make it clear that this is not a case of being overly literal in my interpretation of what seems to be an innocuous figure of speech. Or of being pedantic, an occupational hazard for those of us in the sphere of education. But my starting point is the fact that it really, *really* bothers me when I hear someone say: *It is what it is.*

And I know I'm not alone. *It is what it is* is a sentence that is bound to raise the hackles, or at least raise an eyebrow, of anyone schooled in general semantics. As a saying, it has become very much a 21st century phenomenon, although its origins date back at least to the mid-20th century according to language maven William Safire (2006). He goes on to explain that it is an example of "a deliberate tautology ... designed to define itself by repetition of itself" (p. 22), a figure of speech that he termed a *tautophrase*. As a figure of speech, the phrase is meant to be taken figuratively, not literally, and with varying meanings. For example, Safire identifies it as an alternative to saying *no comment* as a response intended to deflect unwanted questioning. He explains that *no comment* "is rarely used by politicians today because it is too gruff a cliché, slamming the door petulantly, a brushoff by a clumsy amateur. The trick to assertive deflection is in the ducking of a question in a way that sounds forthright" (p. 22). He also quotes the executive editor of the *American Heritage Dictionary* as saying that *it is what it is* represents "a way of expressing philosophical resignation over a disappointment, of saying that the situation just has to be put up with. Athletes will say it about a missed catch or a bad call by the referee; it means that they don't want to dwell on the situation" (p. 22). Along similar lines, the phrase also can be used as a putdown according to Safire, a way of saying something like, *what more can you expect?* of a given person or situation.

Another conscientious objector to *it is what it is* is comedian Jerry Seinfeld. In his 2020 Netflix stand-up comedy special, his routine includes some thoughts on the emptiness of the statement, and others like it:

> But we are all human. Human. The human is **a social species**, as we can see. We tend to congregate, aggregate, and coagulate together. We live here in New York City. That makes no sense. If you take a plane out of New York, and you look down at the city, what do you see around the city? Why, there's nothing but empty, open, beautiful, rolling land out there. Nobody's there! "Let's pack in here, tight!" Uncomfortable, on top of each other, traffic, congestion! That's what we like! Human beings like to be close together because it makes it easier for us to judge and criticize … … the personalities and activities of these humans. We like to give our thoughts, our comments, our opinions. Sometimes, we run out of opinions. We make them up. "It is what it is" is a very popular opinion statement nowadays. I'm sure some idiot said it to you today. You can't get through a day without somebody going, "Well, it is what it is." Why are you alive? To just say air words that fill the room with meaningless sounds? I'd rather someone blew clear air into my face than said, "It is what it is" to me one more time. Just … just come up to me and go … 'Cause I get the same data from that! People like to say those things. "It is what it is." You see,

if you repeat a word twice in a sentence, you can say that with a lot of confidence. "Business is business." "Rules are rules." "Deal's a deal." "When we go in there, as long as we know what's what and who's who, whatever happens, happens, and it is what it is." (Seinfeld, 2020, np)

Seinfeld insightfully concludes with a critique of identity relationships that is entirely consonant with the non-aristotelian approach of general semantics.

And indeed there are many reasons to dislike *it is what it is.* For one, simply put, it has become a cliché, a tired expression, worn out from overuse (which perhaps, hopefully, means that we can expect to see it used less and less frequently in the future). Also, from a relational perspective, *it is what it is* represents a form of rejection, rejecting a topic not by negative evaluation, saying, for example, that it is crazy or stupid talk, but by cutting short the interaction, saying *I don't want to talk about it anymore!* It is an overt dismissal of the content, one that can also function as a covert dismissal of the other person, and the relationship the communicators inhabit (Bateson, 1972, 1979; Watzlawick, Bavelas, & Jackson, 1967). Another reason for disapproving of *it is what it is* is that it reflects a fatalistic worldview, one that denies the possibility of change, and insists on the futility of any attempt to alter our circumstances. It is the present tense counterpart of *what will be will be,* the theme of Doris Day's signature song, "Que Sera, Sera" (music composed by Jay Livingston, lyrics by Ray Evans), although the song is not so much about our inability to change the course of events as it is about our inability to predict what will happen in the future, which would include the effects of our present-day actions; the idea of fate is not necessarily the same as being fatalistic, as fate can refer to the tragedy brought on by hubris (i.e., sealing one's own fate). *It is what it is* is also the third person singular equivalent of the first person declaration, *I am what I am,* or in the immortal words of Popeye the Sailor, *I yam what I yam and that's all I yam!* Here too the inherent fatalism is mitigated by the sense in which it is merely a caution against trying to impose unwanted changes or expectations on another individual, or an acceptance of one's own limitations.

This brings to mind the Book of Exodus and the story of the burning bush, wherein Moses asks God what he should say to the Israelites about who God is. God's reply is

$$\text{אֶהְיֶה אֲשֶׁר אֶהְיֶה}$$

(Ehyeh-Asher-Ehyeh), which is commonly translated as *I am Who I am*, although the preferred translation in Jewish tradition is *I will be Who I will be*. In fact, the Hebrew verb form אֶהְיֶה (Ehyeh) can be understood to mean *I am*, *I will be*, as well as *I was*, which would be consistent with the concept of a transcendent and eternal deity. I think it best, however, to set aside theological considerations, and concentrate on the earthly plane, and the physical universe that we associate with scientific inquiry.

Korzybski's Critique

Whether or not you consider *it is what it is* to be a particularly egregious expression, I think we can all understand that the statement is contradicted by one of Alfred Korzybski's (1933/2023) well known quotes, "whatever one might *say* something *'is'*, it *is not*" (p. 409) or "whatever you say a thing *is*, it *is not*" (p. xxxix [from the Preface to the 5th edition by Robert Pula]), or simply, *whatever you say it is, it isn't*. And if I may be permitted to channel a bit of the spirit of Korzybski, my contribution would be, simply, *it is what it isn't*. Of course, Korzybski is best known for his saying that the "map *is not* the territory" (p. 58), and its counterpart, "the word is not the thing" (p. xlvii [from the Preface to the 4th edition by Russell Meyers]). All of these aphorisms are ways of expressing the principle of non-identity, which is fundamental within Korzybski's non-aristotelian system of general semantics. Korzybski's point is that language leads us to see identity relationships where there are none, to project identity relationships from our symbols onto the physical world, and this leads us to make erroneous assumptions about our environment, to construct maps that do not correspond well to the territory they are intended to depict, maps that therefore can easily lead us astray. For this reason, he singled out the word *is*, and the verb *to be*, as particularly problematic. You might say that, in answer to the question that Shakespeare has Hamlet pose, *to be or not to be*, Korzybski's answer is, **NOT** *to be*.

The verb *to be* is the primary example of a *copula*, a term used in grammar to refer to a verb that connects the subject of a sentence or phrase to its predicate or complement. While other verbs are also considered copular, *to be* is referred to as *the* copula, because it is the most commonly used member of this category. It follows that in place of this basic form of verbal copulation, Korzybski advocated for a more celibate form of language, one that could be termed, *copula-shun*.

This may well serve to remind readers of the infamous remark made by President Bill Clinton, "It depends on what the meaning of *is* is." This was said in testimony he gave to a grand jury, explaining why he was not lying when he told his top aides that there was nothing going on between him and Monica Lewinsky. In that context, it came across as an attempt to evade, deflect, and mislead, as lawyerly manipulation of language, and as inappropriately intellectual and existential—in other words, as stupid talk. But from a general semantics perspective, taken in isolation from the situation, it was a perfectly reasonable and downright insightful point to make. Most people would never think to look up the word *is* in the dictionary. Its meaning seems utterly, obviously self-evident. But if you were to do so, you would find that the word *is* has a great many different definitions listed, either directly or by reference to the word *be*. We can be confident that Clinton was aware of the ambiguous and polysemic quality of language; he also was almost certainly familiar with general semantics itself, as someone who was a student back when S.I. Hayakawa's text, *Language in Thought and Action*, was commonly assigned in secondary school and college, not to mention the fact that he knew Neil Postman personally (and knew the work of media ecologists such as Marshall McLuhan and Walter Ong). I would therefore expect that the former

US president would share my antipathy towards the saying, *it is what it is*, and in fact would agree that, *it is what it isn't!*

I bring this up not to revisit past indiscretions of a former president, which seem almost quaint in light of one of the more recent occupants of the oval office, but rather to underscore the fact that the verb *to be* has many meanings and functions, and they are not all created equal. That is why Korzybski lamented the fact that some perfectly benign meanings are locked together with the problematic ones in the same linguistic prison house of *is*. Indeed, his main beef was with two particular meanings of the word *is*, primarily what is known as the *is* of identity, and secondarily the *is* of predication. As Koryzbski explained in his magnum opus *Science and Sanity*, originally published in 1933:

> The 'is' of identity plays a great havoc with our *s.r.* [semantic reactions], as any 'identity' is structurally false to fact. An infant does not know and cannot know that. In his life, the 'is' of identity plays an important semantic role, which, if not checked intelligently, becomes a pernicious semantic factor in his grown-up reactions, which preserve the infantile character and with which *adult* adjustment and semantic health is impossible. The infant begins to speak and again he is trained in the 'is' of identity. Symbols are identified with un-speakable actions, events and objects under penalty of pain or even death. The magic of words begins its full sway. As a rule, parental, crude disciplining of the infant, particularly in former days, trained the *s.r.* [semantic reactions] of the infant again in the delusional 'is' of identity. The results are semantically and structurally very far-reaching and are found in modern mythologies, militarism, the prevailing economic and social systems, the control by fear (be it 'hell' or machine guns), illusory gold standards, hunger, [etc.].
>
> Experience shows that such identification of symbols with the un-speakable levels works very well with animals. With man, it leads only to the misuse of the human nervous system,

semantic disturbances of evaluation, and the prevailing unstable animalistic systems in practically all fields, resulting in the general chaos in human affairs.

It should be noted that the 'is' of predication also expresses a sort of *partial identity*, leading to primitive anthropomorphism and general confusion of orders of abstraction. (Korzybski, 1933/2023, p. 202).

M(is)taken Identity

Korzybski's primary concern is with what might be considered a case of mistaken identity, which is to say, as previously noted, that human beings are mistaken insofar as we believe that there is such a thing as identity, at least outside of the symbolic realm. In the language of algebra, saying, $X=2$, means that the variable X is defined as the quantity two, which can simply be stated as *X is two*. In the more basic language of arithmetic, we say that *two plus two is four*, and there is nothing wrong with this statement, insofar as we understand the word *is* to take the place of the mathematical relationship otherwise represented by the term *equals*. Korzybski had no issues with mathematics as a symbol system; in fact, stemming from his background in science and engineering, he favored it for its ability to represent physical reality with great precision. The problem, which he linked to Aristotelian logic, was the tendency to apply the concept of equality outside of a quantitative code, to real world phenomena. Aristotle codified this as the *law of identity*, which is a much more formal way of saying *it is what it is*, or *things are what they are*, or as Gertrude Stein famously uttered, *a rose is a rose is a rose is a rose*. I hasten to add that Korzybski was well aware of the value of poetry, and was not concerned with producing literary criticism of "Sacred Emily" or any other of Stein's compositions. Rather, the problem is when such statements are put forth as descriptions of the world, the equivalent of saying that all roses are alike. Admittedly, for some purposes, we may treat roses as interchangeable, but scientifically, no two roses are exactly alike. And it is not just that roses resemble snowflakes in their formal composition. Rather, it is that no two cows are alike, no matter whether we treat them as if they are. No two people are alike. No two copies of the same book are alike—we may mass produce them so that their differences are all but unnoticeable, but minute differences remain. No two chairs are alike—Korzybski reportedly once sat on a chair that collapsed and said, *aha!* *a chair is not a chair*. Simply put, there are no identity relationships in nature.

By the same token, nature is non-additive. One plus one equals two arithmetically, but add one cloud to another and you do not necessarily get two clouds, or one cloud that is twice as big. And parents know all too well that when you have one child and add another, you do not simply get twice as much childrearing to deal with, but instead much more to handle, at times more than you can handle. Long ago Robert Moses discovered that when you have traffic jams, building more roads and bridges does not necessarily reduce the amount of traffic, as you would expect if the real world worked in additive fashion; in fact, it results in even more traffic, not less. This is a basic concept in systems theory, that systems do not work in additive fashion, which is the basis of the saying that *the whole is greater than the sum of its parts*, or more accurately, that *the whole is* other *than the sum of its parts*. Korzybski's work on general semantics anticipated systems theory, which is why Ludwig von Bertalanffy (1969) referred to it as *general* system theory (or *general* systems theory), following the example of *general* semantics.

Even more fundamentally, Aristotelian logic's law of identity is expressed as A *equals A*, meaning *a thing is what it is*, essentially saying that *it is what it is*, and this suggests stasis and permanence. Think about two unopened bottles of natural spring water, say each one marked one liter. We may consider them to be equal and interchangeable, but do they have the exact same amount of water? The answer, of course, is no. When it comes to counting, we can say that each bottle counts as one bottle, and since one equals one, each water bottle counts the same as every other bottle, for the purposes of counting (e.g., when taking inventory). But measurement, by way of contrast, is always an approximation. There is no exact measurement of one liter, which is why in measurement we calculate the greatest margin of error. Anthony Wilden (1980) uses counting as an example of a *digital* operation that is associated with an either-or logic, either it is one bottle or two bottles. Measurement, on the other hand, is understood to be an *analogical* operation, one that is instead associated with a more-or-less logic, each bottle containing more or less one liter, but never exactly the same amount, even if the differences are as small as to be on the molecular level. But then, take one of those bottles in isolation, and ask, does it contain the same amount of water from one moment to the next? The answer is no, because molecules of water are always evaporating and condensing, so the exact amount of water is always in flux. This is what 20th century physics revealed about the nature of reality, that it is dynamic, always changing. That the universe is not made up of things, but rather of events taking place in spacetime. That in place of stasis we have process. That even an equilibrium is dynamic. That what seems like *stasis* is actually *homeostasis*. That all phenomena are forms of energy, and on a subatomic level phenomena are packets of energy we call particles (or strings), sometimes flowing as waves. And that change is the only constant. Nothing is identical to anything else, and nothing is identical to itself. Which brings us back to the idea that the verb *to be* provides a false impression of reality. In philosophical terms, there is no *be-ing*, only *be-coming*.

Opening the Doors of Perception

One of the themes closely associated with Korzybski is the need to be able to set aside language as a medium that separates us from our environment, and thereby get closer to an unfiltered experience of reality. The goal would be to open the *doors of perception*, to use the phrase coined by William Blake, and adopted by Aldous Huxley (1954), whose writings were influenced by general semantics. This idea became particularly popular in the post war era, with various methods being employed, psychedelic drugs being one of them, transcendental meditation and eastern mysticism and spirituality being another, both also linked to various forms of therapy and human potential movements. As explained by the psychotherapist and founder of transactional analysis, Eric Berne, in his popular book, *Games People Play* (1964),

> Awareness means the capacity to see a coffeepot and hear the birds sing in one's own way, and not the way one was taught. It may be assumed on good grounds that seeing and hearing have a different quality for infants than for grownups, and that they are more esthetic and less intellectual in the first years of life. A little boy sees and hears birds with delight. Then the "good father" comes along and feels he should "share" the experience and help his son "develop." He says: "That's a jay, and this is a sparrow." The moment the little boy is concerned with which is a jay and which is a sparrow, he can no longer see the birds or hear them sing. He has to see and hear them the way his father wants him to. Father has good reasons on his side, since few people can afford to go through life listening to the birds sing, and the sooner the little boy starts his "education" the better. Maybe he will be an ornithologist when he grows up. A few people, however, can still see and hear in the old way. But most of the members of the human race have lost the capacity to be painters, poets or musicians, and are not left the option of seeing and hearing directly even if they can afford to; they must get it secondhand. (pp. 78–79)

Apart from better adjustment to reality, there is also the idea that capturing the openness of the prelinguistic state is the key to creativity. This applies to science as well as art, as famously expressed by the physicist J. Robert Oppenheimer: "There are children playing in the streets who could solve some of my top problems in physics, because they have modes of sensory perception that I lost long ago." The fact that artists, or at least some artists, never lost those modes, or were able to reclaim them, led Marshall McLuhan (1964) to conclude that art can serve as an antienvironment to our standard, linguistically mediated environment, and that education should be grounded in art as a way to train our senses and hone our perceptions.

Further, whereas Korzybski said that *the word is not the thing*, the anthropologist Dorothy Lee (1959) framed the relationship somewhat differently, moving the concept of the *thing* from one side of the equation to another, arguing that it is not part of our environment, but rather part of the symbolic realm. As she explains it,

> According to the classical view, the word is not the *thing*. This object that I hold in my hand is independent of the name I give it. It *is* not a pencil: I only assign to it the name pencil. What *it is*, is assumed to be independent of what *I call it*. Pencil is only a sound-complex, a word for the reality, the *thing*. But the sound aspect of "pencil" is only one aspect of it. When I call this "pencil," I also classify it, as a substantive, a noun; I separate it as other than the fingers it elongates. Is it a thing before I call it a *pencil*?
>
> If it is not, then I am not "applying" a name to an already existing thing. This physical reality, this formless mass or energy, or set of relations, is delimited, is given form and substance, becomes the *thing* pencil, only by my calling it a pencil. In naming it, I give it recognition and a status in the categories of experienced reality. Calling it a pencil is the symbolic process through which I have created it; so that its name, or rather its naming, is a necessary part of itself, without which it is not this *thing*. And conversely, its name cannot be separated from it as a self-contained element, it has no independent existence as symbol to be applied to an already existing *thing*. (p. 80)

Lee (1959) goes on to conclude, "The word and the thing are not discrete elements to be related by the speaker; they are interdependent, incapable of existence apart from and without the act of the individual"

(p. 80). Her argument, consistent with the approach known as linguistic relativism (aka the Sapir-Whorf Hypothesis), is that language directs our perception, indicating what to pay attention to, and therefore what parts of our environment are isolated and identified as objects, or things. To use the terms associated with art and perception favored by McLuhan (1964), language influences the figure-ground dichotomy of visual perception, so that whatever has a name will stand out for us as a distinct figure, as opposed to all else that blends into the background and fades from conscious awareness. Naming any aspect of our environment reifies the *figure*, transforming it into a *thing*. I do want to stress that while Lee and Koryzybski may seem at odds with one another, the difference is not all that significant (and I am certain that Korzybski would concede the point to Lee), in that they both agree on the basic principle of non-identity, that what we describe with words is not equal to what we perceive with our senses, and that what we perceive with our senses is not equal to what is actually going on in the environment.

Naming, in the sense of making a statement along the lines of, *that is a jay*, and *this is a sparrow*, is a powerful tool, but like all tools, technologies, and media, there are costs that we pay in exchange for their benefits (see, for example, Strate, 2014, 2017b). A classic example of naming can be found in the Book of Genesis, when Adam gives the animals their names. In the words of the King James translation, "And out of the ground the Lord God formed every beast of the field, and every fowl of the air; and brought them unto Adam to see what he would call them: and whatsoever Adam called every living creature, that was the name thereof" (2:19). This passage expresses the power of naming, the sense of control it provides, in its expression of human dominion over nature. But this also reflects the downside of naming, in its relation to power, as well as the fact that it can be a contested activity, at times hotly debated, even to the extent of leading to violent exchanges. Naming has historically been a tool of conquest and imperialism, for example when New Amsterdam was changed to New York, as well as an assertion of identity, for example when Constantinople was renamed Istanbul, or the name Burma was replaced by Myanmar.

It is true that scientific naming is a tool that allows for greater precision than everyday language, as in a statement such as, *the honey bee is Apis melifera L.*, which is an abbreviated way of saying that *the scientific name for the honey bee is Apis melifera L.* But it can also provide a false sense of understanding, and with it comfort, even control, when, say, a medical name is substituted for a symptom that was previously expressed in plain language, thereby substituting for any genuine explanation of phenomena. This sort of thing was satirized by the playwright Molière in *The Imaginary Invalid*, in which a group of physicians attribute the fact that opium makes people drowsy to its *virtus dormitiva*, a Latin phrase translated as its *dormitive virtue* or *dormitive principle*. This points to the tautological quality of naming, essentially saying that opium makes you sleepy because it has the characteristic of making you sleepy. Once again, *a rose is a rose is a rose is a rose*.

The Numbing Blow of Naming

When someone asks, *who are you?*, typically the first *I am ...* answer that we give is to state our name. *I am Lance Strate* is a statement of identity in more ways than one, as it suggests that I am the same person I was when I was born, the same all throughout the past, and the same into as much of a future as I have left. It is also sobering to think that most of us go by names that we did not choose, that were chosen for us, either before we were born or soon thereafter. McLuhan (1964) quipped, that "the name of a man is a numbing blow from which he never recovers" (p. 32). He perhaps meant that that particular manifestation of the *is* of identity numbs us into believing that, *I yam what I yam and that's all I yam*, which is to say that our personality and personal identity is set at birth, irrevocable and unchangeable. The result is what McLuhan referred to as *narcissus narcosis*, mistaking, in this case, the name and not the reflection for the person it represents. By being named, we are numbed to our prelinguistic state of mind. The effect is narcotic, and dormitive, turning us into somnambulistic creatures, sleepwalking through our own lives. The title character of the

British TV series from the sixties, *The Prisoner*, famously declared, *I am not a number! I am a free man!*, in protest against bureaucratic control and captivity. But substituting his name, which the series never reveals, would not make him free from the tyranny of the verb *to be*, and what might be termed the *am* of identity.

You can change your name or adopt a nickname, of course, but as long as the new name is expressed via the *is* of identity, then the structure of the relationship, and its problematic nature, remains unchanged. This is also true of an alias. Another example would be the statement, *Lewis Carroll is Charles Lutwidge Dodgson*. This of course is a shorthand way of saying that Lewis Carroll is the pen name of Charles Lutwidge Dodgson, more precise and less absolute, but still in the realm of identity. Are they really the same? Or is Lewis Carroll, in effect, a fictional character, arguably a metanarrator, created by Dogson?

From a general semantics perspective, it is always helpful to think about alternatives. Instead of saying, *I am Lance Strate*, I can say, *my name is Lance Strate*, which still involves the *is* of identity, but at least removes it from my essential being. Better yet would be to say that *I am known as Lance Strate*, even better to say, *I am called Lance Strate*, as that emphasizes the speech act of *calling* and *being called*. It can be presented as a command, as in, *call me Ishmael*, or a request, as in, *you can call me Ray, or you can call me Jay*, and so on, or if you prefer a musical version, *you can call me Al*. And it can be turned back in on myself, as in, *me, a name, I call myself*. But by using the formulation of *I am called* rather than *I am*, we see a shift in emphasis from an internalized, intensional orientation, to an externalized, extensional orientation. In French, it is possible to say *je suis Charlie*, a statement of identity and solidarity, but it is perhaps more commonplace to say *je m'appelle Charles*, from the Old French root that gave us the English word *appellation*. And given that we typically take our last names from our family, it might be said that the appellation does not fall far from the tree. As for the flower, *a rose is a rose*, would be more accurate if it were rendered as, *a rose is whatever is named a rose*, or, *a rose is the name of a rose, or a rose is what we call a rose*.

Of course, the verb *to be* is still present in statements such as, *I am called Lance Strate*, and *he is called Ishmael*, but as a helping verb, an auxiliary verb, and Korzybski had no objection to those meanings of the verb *to be*.

The Tyranny of Definitions

Naming is closely associated with definitions. For example, saying that domesticated female cattle that provide us with milk and beef *are* cows means nothing more than that the animal is *called* a cow, that it is *assigned the name* of cow, that that is how we define the word *cow*. Similarly, when I stated that a copula is a verb that connects the subject of sentence or phrase to its predicate or complement, I was only providing a definition of a term, much like a dictionary does. In this instance, the statement is simply saying that *it is what it is by definition*, or put another way, that this is how we define the term *copula*. It follows that definitions are essentially tautological (Condon, 1985) in that they basically say that a term *is what it is*, meaning that it *is* what it is defined as. Definitions gain authority from the *is* of identity, and also from anonymity, as they often are put forth without attribution or authorship, for example in the way that they are presented in the dictionary. In this regard, it is worth noting that the 1964 film by Jean Luc Goddard, *Alphaville*, in depicting a dystopian society, dominated by a computer located in a fictionalized Institute of General Semantics, reveals that the book that the inhabitants refer to as "the bible" is in fact a dictionary based on Orwellian principles. In this context, it is also worth noting that definitions can be used for propaganda purposes, for example via the technique referred to as *persuasive definition*, in which a single definition is put forth as the only possible definition of a term. Neil Postman (1995) refers to the *tyranny of definitions*, invoking the explanation provided by I.A. Richards:

> We want to do something and a definition is a means of doing it. If we want certain results, then we must use certain meanings

(or definitions). But no definition has any authority apart from a purpose, or to bar us from other purposes. And yet they endlessly do so. Who can doubt that we are often deprived of very useful thoughts merely because the words which might express them are being temporarily preempted by other meanings? Or that a development is often frustrated merely because we are sticking to a former definition of no service to the new purpose. (quoted in Postman, 1995, p. 183)

One answer is to invoke the general semantics-based advice of Wendell Johnson (1946), and employ operational definitions, that is, definitions that are understood to be specific to a particular context, as in the phrase "for the purposes of this study" used in scholarly and scientific research; operational definitions are concrete and specific, and as much as possible specify the procedures or operations to be used in conjunction with the term. In this way, rather than saying what a copula *is*, I would qualify the definition by saying that *in this context* or *for our purposes*, the term copula *is defined as* a verb that connects the subject of sentence or phrase to its predicate or complement. Operational definitions open the door to alternatives, which Postman (1995) suggests is the answer to definition tyranny. As he explains,

> In an effort to clear us of confusion (or ignorance) about the meaning of a word, does anyone ask, What is *a* definition of this word? Just about always, the way of putting the question is, What is *the* definition of this word? The difference between *a* and *the* in this context is vast, and I have no choice but to blame the schools for the mischief created by an inadequate understanding of what a definition is. From the earliest grades through graduate school, students are given definitions and, with few exceptions, are not told whose definitions they are, for what purposes they were invented, and what alternative definitions might serve equally as well. The result is that students come to believe that definitions are *not* invented, that they are

not even human creations; that, in fact, they are—how shall I say it?—part of the natural world, like clouds, trees, and stars. (p. 172)

Categorical Confusion

Definitions sometimes incorporate categorization, and whether part of a definition or not, categorization was also a concern for Korzybski. Consider a statement like, *Donald is a criminal*. Such a statement would indicate that Donald is a member of the category referred to as criminals, but in Aristotelian fashion, we tend to interpret it as meaning that Donald *equals* criminal, a false equivalence. On one side of the equation, it suggests that all that we associate with being a criminal applies to Donald, all the time and everywhere, so that no matter what he is doing, he is breaking the law. On the other side of the equation, the statement suggests that everything we know about Donald is characteristic of everyone who is identified as a criminal. This is where the general semantics principle of *non-allness* serves as a remedy, reminding us that we can never say all there is to say about anything or anyone. Donald may indeed be a criminal, but he may also be a father, a son, a husband, a boss, a reality TV star, even a former president. Such statements also can lead us into what Korzybski (1933/2023) termed a *two-valued orientation*, otherwise known as *either-or thinking*, for example by saying that either Donald *is* a president or he *is* a criminal, rather than allowing for the possibility of *both-and* statements (ill-considered Supreme Court decisions not withstanding). This follows the Aristotelian laws of logic that are linked to the law of identity, specifically the law of non-contradiction and the law of the excluded middle. These kinds of statements also convey a sense of timelessness and permanence, obscuring the fact that everything is always changing over time. Donald may be a criminal now, but he was not born a criminal, gaining the status of *criminal* is a process, a becoming not a being; further, after being convicted and serving out his sentence in prison, he may be released and therefore, by legal definition, would no longer be a criminal.

A statement like *the dog is a pet* obscures the fact that there are in fact canines that are feral or undomesticated and wild. Or it may suggest that all dogs are friendly to humans, and safe to pet. The concern about the word *is* is intimately related to the need for consciousness of abstracting that forms the basis of Korzybski's discipline of general semantics. A statement like *Donald is a criminal*, or *dogs are pets*, are examples of the process of abstracting, which involves making generalizations. This is a form of stereotyping in its most basic sense, which is simply putting things into categories, and also entails leaving out details and differences regarding the members of the category. We can see this in action in the form of the syllogism associated with Aristotelian logic. So, for example, when we say, *All men are mortal, Socrates is a man, therefore Socrates is mortal*, we are saying that Socrates is a member of the general category of men, or human beings to use contemporary, non-sexist language, and that whatever is characteristic of the category as a whole is characteristic of all of its individual members. And it is important to emphasize that there is nothing wrong with making generalizations; the trick is to be aware that that is what we are doing. And to understand that how we go about abstracting is subjective, in the sense that we make a choice as to which categories to put things into. I can say that dogs are pets, in which case I identify them with cats, and parrots and parakeets, and tropical fish, frogs and turtles, iguanas, snakes, and even tarantulas, and emphasize whatever characteristics all of these animals have in common. Or I can say that dogs are mammals, in which case I identify them with lions, and tigers, and bears, and human beings, and emphasize whatever characteristics all of these species have in common. The problem of identity in this instance is the problem of stereotyping, or rather the many problems with stereotyping, which can include

1. that generalizations made regarding the category are incorrect or inaccurate or apply only to some members of the category
2. that whatever category something or someone is identified with excludes other possible categories that can also be used and may be equally or more relevant

3. that any act of categorization involves leaving out details specific to the individual member of the category, and that distinguish one member of the category from another, that therefore correspond to the subject's unique individuality and/or the unique event in spacetime

Korzybski's concept of abstracting, illustrated by his famous structural differential model (see p. 56), is the key to understanding the problem inherent in categorization, understanding that *the category is not the category member*, an idea that originates with the theory of logical types put forth by Alfred North Whitehead and Bertrand Russell (1925–1927). Whenever we categorize, whatever it is that we are categorizing most certainly *is what it isn't*. The problem is further exacerbated by the fact that, in accordance with the general semantics principle of *self-reflexiveness*, we can have categories of things, and categories of categories, and categories of categories of categories, and so on. I can say that dogs are mammals, and mammals are animals, and animals are living things, in each case equating a category on a lower level of abstracting with one that is on a higher level, and thereby taking us further away from the external environment and the concrete level of prelinguistic perception.

Problematic Predications

Categories are nouns, but the criticism of the verb *to be* extends to adjectives as well, to statements where the predicate linked to the word *is* is some kind of descriptive attribute or quality. In the classic syllogism I previously cited, the first premise, that all men are mortal, is an example of this type of statement. Based on Aristotelian logic, the statement could be understood as an equation in which the category referred to as *men* (which is to say, *human beings*) equals the attribute termed *mortality*. The equation forms the basis of the metonymic usage of the word *mortal* to refer to a human being, used by way of contrast to conceptions of divine or supernatural entities. The either-or logic at work here suggests that if there are mortals, their counterpart would have to be immortals. This manifestation of the equation also disregards the fact that mortality is a characteristic of all life, not just our species. And while the basic idea that mortality is an inherent concept of all human beings is not controversial, following Karl Popper (2002) it is not a statement that can be *proven* to be true by empirical means, because that would require verifying that every human being who ever was, is, or will be, has died, which cannot be known as long as long as human beings continue to exist in the future (and when there are none of us left, will there be anyone else with the capability to draw that conclusion?).

Taking another example, if I say that *Donald is evil*, once again when engaged in Aristotelian thinking, I have posited an equation in which Donald *equals* evil, so that all that Donald is *is* evil, that the characteristic of being evil applies to him fully and completely, suggesting as well that everything about Donald applies to our understanding of evil as a quality. Whatever you or I may feel about that particular equation, we can see where it becomes especially problematic, and potentially a textbook case of a Batesonian double bind (Bateson, 1972, 1979; Watzlawick et al, 1967), when a parent says to a young child, *you are bad!* That statement conveys the sense that you are inherently bad, entirely bad, always and everywhere bad. That parents should not communicate to children in this way was established long ago. A better way to say it is, *you did a bad thing!* This way, the parent is no longer using the word *is*, and no longer providing negative evaluation of the child as a person, instead showing disapproval towards a specific action that the child performed; it is also clearly easier to change *what* we *do* than to change *who* we *are*. Even better, however, would be to say, *what you did made me angry*, or *what you did made me sad*, which eliminates the quality of *badness* altogether, and has parents owning their reactions rather than displacing them onto the child.

Modifiers such as adjectives and adverbs are transformed by the verb *to be*. When we have a phrase such as *good person*, the adjective is closely tied to the noun it modifies. It may not be a complete sentence, but the rules about what does and does not constitute a complete sentence are arbitrary, having emerged out of the typographic media environment and its print culture, and established by prescriptive grammarians (Postman & Weingartner, 1966). The rule they put forth may say that a complete sentence must have a subject and predicate, but then again the subject can be implied in the case of commands such as "Go!" And as Christine Nystrom (2021), drawing on George Herbert Mead (1934), points out, when a toddler in an early stage of language acquisition says something like, *Juice!*, there is a complete thought involved, and the single word actually means the entire sentence, *I want to drink some juice! Give me some juice to drink!* What this means is that further development in language acquisition, moving from the use of single words to the formation of sentences, does not involve adding more words so much as it is based on the breaking apart of holistic concepts expressed via single words such as, *Juice!*

Breaking concepts apart, especially when the verb *to be* is involved, has further implications. If I say *good person*, the meaning is eminently clear despite being a sentence fragment, the context clarifying whether I am referring to a specific individual or an entire category (a more common example would be a phrase like *good boy!*, used as expression of approval in regard to a pet, or a person). Consider what happens, though, when I instead produce a sentence using the word *is*, and say, *that person is good.* I have separated the modifier from the modified, and given it its own independent existence. In this way, I imply that the concept of *good* can be considered independently of any noun; I can even turn it into a noun in its own right by asking, *what is good?* Or *what is the good?* I think it obvious that this opens the door to the kind of abstract thinking characteristic of philosophical discourse. General semantics warns against getting lost in high level abstractions and losing sight of their concrete connection to the human lifeworld, and we can see how this can be an occupational hazard for intellectuals, and how the *is of identity* and the *is of predication* is implicated when this happens.

At the same time, Wendell Johnson (1946) warns against dead level abstracting, which is as much a problem when we only talk about specifics and are incapable of generalizing, as when we only deal with highly abstract terms. Science is based on our ability to generalize, to form theories and hypotheses based on empirical evidence. Consider adjectives relating to color. I can use the phrase *blue sky* to refer to the sky, in contrast to grey skies that are going to clear up, or in parallel to a phrase like *blue suede shoes*. But when I say that *the sky is blue* and *these shoes are blue*, I am implying that there is this attribute of blueness that exists independently of both sky and shoe. Granted, the word guides my perception, so I pay attention to the color blue in general, whereas for individuals who use the Russian language, which has two different words, one for light blue and one for dark blue, they see things a bit differently. It is not that I do not notice the differences, but that they do not register as significant, and neurological research shows that brain activity differs for English and Russian speakers when shown the different shades of blue (Boroditsky, 2011). Nevertheless, in suggesting that there is such a thing as the color blue (or colors light blue and dark blue) independent of anything that is identified as being blue, that instead there is an objective phenomenon we refer to as *blue*, language opens the door to scientific research regarding color, research on light, optics, and perception.

Along similar lines, words indicating quantity originally only existed as adjectives. You could have two seashells, or two cows, or two pebbles, but not *two* itself as something separate and distinct from specific items—even the operations for counting would depend on what was being counted, and differ accordingly (Goody, 1977). The invention of writing had much to do with turning numbers into nouns, as the original technique of one-to one correspondence between notational marks and what they represent (as in tally marks) was replaced by separate characters for numbers and objects. The earlier method would be to repeat the character for seashells, or cows, or pebbles, however many times to match the number of items, so that if you had two seashells you would make two marks that stood for a seashell, and if you had five cows you would make five cow marks; when different, separate characters were adopted to indicate quantity, *numerals* in other words, the number was separated from whatever was being counted, leading to the idea that numbers have their own independent existence (Schmandt-Besserat, 1996). We can therefore contemplate the quantity of five, the numerical value of five, as an abstract concept and in effect a *thing* unto itself. This opened the door to mathematics, something that Korzybski would no doubt approve of. At the same time, it led to superstitions about numbers, to numerology and *triskaidekaphobia*, the fear of the number thirteen, which has had a significant effect on the numbering of floors in buildings, among other things. More significant is how numbers become implicated in the tyranny of definitions, and forms of reification, for example in the use of test scores to determine college admissions, or IQ scores to determine whether individuals must be legally institutionalized (Gould, 1992; Postman, 1976, 1992, 1995). As the saying often attributed to Mark Twain maintains, *there are three kinds of lies: lies, damned lies, and statistics.* The tendency to identify just about everything as a number, including human beings, is very much a characteristic of modernity, associated with imprisonment, as in Victor Hugo's *Les Misérables*, in which Jean Valjean is Prisoner 24601, a designation highlighted in the popular musical adaptation; arguably the most infamous examples was the tattooing of numbers on those imprisoned in German concentration camps during the Second World War. Associated with bureaucracy as well, criticism of this practice was reflected in the cry, *I am not a number! I am a free man!* from the aforementioned television series, *The Prisoner*. Quantification is not without its benefits, as it uncovers heretofore unnoticed risks, albeit at the cost of making us risk-aversive (Perkinson 1996). Through calculation, we are able to increase efficiency in ways not possible previously, but this too leads to the rise of a technical imperative in which efficiency crowds out any other criteria and all human value (Ellul, 1964; Strate, 2011b, 2014).

Metaphors Be With You

So far, I have discussed Korzybski's criticism of the *is of identity* and the *is of predication*, as manifested in statements involving names, definitions, categories, and attributes. At this point, I believe that the unusual case of metaphor deserves some mention. It is certainly the case that statements involving metaphor make use of the verb *to be*, for example in the line by Robert Burns, *my love is like a red, red rose*. In the special case of metaphor known as simile, the fact that the statement is an analogy rather than a digital equation is eminently clear. Saying that my love *is like* a rose indicates some sort of similarity, but at the same time admits of the understanding that my love *is not* a rose. Metaphor is typically referred to as a *comparison*, which is different than an equation, and it is understood that the comparison is between two things that are not alike. It would not be a metaphor if I said that *my love is like a friend with benefits*, for example, because the two are not that far apart conceptually. Removing the qualifying *like* or *as* of simile, an overtly metaphorical statement is still recognizable as an analogy. Saying my love *is* a rose or in more familiar terms, my love *is* a delicate flower, does not lead all but the most literally-minded into making Aristotelian assumptions about my having a passionate relationship with a plant. We typically understand that the language is figurative, so that such statements are not problematic for general semantics. Simply put, a metaphor is a way of saying that *it is what it isn't*; conversely, *it is what it is* constitutes a truism, and therefore could be considered an *antimetaphor*.

We can also take into consideration the metaphor theory developed by George Lakoff and Mark Johnson (1980), and further elaborated by Ray Gozzi (1999), and recognize that metaphors can be deeply embedded in language, which can in fact lead to issues regarding identity relationships. For example, while we would expect individuals to recognize that the saying, *time is money*, is a metaphor, most of us are unaware of how the metaphor operates in our language and affects us without us being aware of it. The metaphor is at work, and working us over, when we talk about *buying* time, *borrowing* time, *investing* time, *lending* time, and *spending* time, as well as *spending* time *profitably*, not to mention asking if it is *worth* your while. Through these and other expressions, we not only compare time to money, we conceptualize time as money, and experience time as money. In this case, invoking the *is* of identity could actually serve to make us aware that we are using a metaphor, and that, in fact, *it is what it isn't*. Consider the following imaginary interaction:

Bud: Lou, you really need to buy yourself some time! Right now, you're living on borrowed time! You need to start spending your time profitably, and work on something that's worth your while. You gotta just start investing your time wisely.
Lou: Are you saying that time is money?
Bud: Yes!
Lou: But is time really money? Do you really believe that?
Bud: No, of course not. It's just a figure of speech.
Lou: You mean a metaphor?
Bud: Yeah, that's right, that's what it is.
Lou: Well, are there other ways we can talk about time that doesn't compare it to money?
Bud: I suppose so. I'd have to think about it.

And we will leave off here, with the understanding that, when it comes to metaphors, we can consider what the similarities might be, but also what the differences are, and importantly, what alternate metaphors we might turn to. But the point here is that in the case of metaphor, in contrast to the other cases discussed here, the use of the verb *to be* can paradoxically bring home the non-identity inherent in the analogical statement.

~~IS~~

~~BE~~

~~AM~~

~~ARE~~

~~WAS~~

~~BEEN~~

~~WERE~~

~~BEING~~

Controversies Over Copula-Shun

As I have taken pains to emphasize, Korzybski was only concerned with certain particular uses of the word *is* and the verb *to be*. And he proposed a variety of techniques to try to cope with the misleading effects of language on our thinking, such as *indexing* (time$_1$ is not time$_2$), *dating* (money^{1980} is not money^{2020}), and *etc* (to indicate that all statements are incomplete). He also suggested substituting for and otherwise avoiding the use of the word *is* and the verb *to be* some of time, in some instances. But within the general semantics community, the practice that I have termed *copula-shun* was taken to an extreme by one of Korzybski's students, David Bourland. Bourland (1965/1966) proposed the complete elimination of the verb *to be* from the English language, not just the *is of identity* and the *is of predication*, but every usage of the word *is*, and *are*, *am*, *was*, *were*, *be*, *being*, and *been*, including the contractions that incorporate them. He referred to this new kind of language as E-Prime, short for English-Prime. In support of this initiative, Bourland invoked not only Korzybski, but the pragmatist philosopher George Santayana (1923), who famously wrote:

> The little word *is* has its tragedies; it marries and identifies different things with the greatest innocence; and yet not two are ever identical, and if therein lies the charm of wedding them and calling them one, therein too lies the danger. Whenever I use the word *is*, except in sheer tautology, I deeply misuse it; and when I discover my error, the world seems to fall asunder and the members of my family no longer know one another. (p. 71)

Notably, and sensibly, Santayana falls short of the complete and total ban on the verb *to be* required for E-Prime. Bourland also cited the 19th century logician Augustus De Morgan (1847), who wrote,

> The most difficult inquiry which any one can propose to himself is to find out what any thing *is*: in all probability we do not know

what we are talking about when we ask such a question. The philosophers of the middle ages were much concerned with the *is*, or *essence*, of things: they argued to their own minds, with great justice, that if they could only find out what a thing is, they should found out all about it: they tried, and failed. Their successors, taking their warning by example, have inverted the proposition; and have satisfied themselves that the only way of finding what a thing is, lies in finding what we can about it; that modes of relation and connexion are all we know of the essence of any thing; in short, that the proverb, 'tell me who you are with, and I will tell you what you are,' applies as much to the nature of things as to the characters of men. We are apt to think that we know more of the essence of objects than of ideas; or rather, of ideas which have an objective source, than of those which are the consequences of the mind's action upon them. I doubt whether the reverse be not the case: at any rate, when we content ourselves with inquiry into properties and relations, we have certain knowledge upon our most abstract ideas. (p. 170)

De Morgan's primary concern is with symbolic logic and not natural language, and therefore he offers no practical solution, nor even a blanket criticism of the use of the verb *to be* outside of philosophical investigation. The important point, however, is that criticism of the copula did not originate with Korzybski, or Santayana, or De Morgan for that matter. Indeed, according to Theodor Gomperz (1901), the ancient Greek sophist Lycophron, a student of the sophist known as Gorgias (best known to us via the vehemently anti-sophist dialogue of Plato, 1971, that features his name), "avoided the use of the verb 'to be' altogether, even as a copula" (p. 493), a practice that Gorgias himself may have initiated (whether this means that E-Prime is a form of sophistry remains to be determined). The practice outlined by Bourland, gained some popularity after being featured in an article in *The Atlantic* magazine by Cullen Murphy (1992), "To Be in Their Bonnets," but it has also been a source of controversy even within the general semantics community, as reflected in a special issue of the journal *ETC: A Review of General Semantics* (Klein, 1992) devoted to the topic, published in 1992. E-Prime advocates contributing to that publication were ardent in their advocacy of the approach, arguing on behalf of its efficacy as a means of instilling a non-aristotelian mindset. Moreover, a number of works have been published in E-Prime, including three anthology collections co-edited by Bourland (Bourland & Johnston, 1991, 1997; Bourland, Klein, & Johnston, 1994). Other major works composed in this mode include, *The New American Standard Bible in E-Prime*, prepared by general semanticist David F. Maas (2011), and available online via the website of the Institute of General Semantics, and notably, the nonfiction work *Quantum Psychology* by Robert Anton Wilson (1990). Proponents of E-Prime also include the noted psychotherapist Albert Ellis who explained that he "wrote several books and articles in E-prime" and that it "discourages inaccurate and self-defeating use of language," although as an author he also "found that it interferes somewhat with readability" (Ellis, 2001, p. 2).

I myself wrote an essay in E-Prime (Strate, 2003; reprinted in Strate, 2011b), excepting for the quotes I included in the piece as it would not be appropriate to alter the words of others; it was an interesting exercise, albeit one that I do not care to repeat. Contrary to Ellis, however, there is an argument to be made that E-Prime results in a better, more active and engaging style of writing than we might otherwise obtain. Andrea Johnson (1992) discusses a writing exercise she learned from general semanticist Kenneth G. Johnson, in which students are asked to write a one-page autobiography in E-Prime, and states that many students reported that it was one of the most valuable assignments she gave, in regard to both writing and the kind of self improvement Ellis referred to. In a class that I teach, I use a somewhat different E-Prime exercise, where I ask students to take a paragraph from a nonfiction source such as a news report and rewrite it in E-Prime. The objective is to make students aware of the subliminal quality of our use of the verb *to be*, and how it affects our descriptions and reporting. E-Prime also has something to offer when it comes to creative writing. Risa Kaparo (1992) particularly points to its importance for poetry, suggesting that,

> the poem provides an environment in which the reader can enter a first person, subjective awareness of the "here/now," the fluctuations of feelings and sensations, needs and desires, imagination and intuition. In this way, the writing creates a context in which the reader can extend his or her awareness, just like walking in a garden might nourish within awareness a growing range of sensitivities that enrich a vital, felt-sense of aliveness. (pp. 180–181)

She goes on to quote Ernest Fenollosa's essay, "The Chinese Character as a Medium for Poetry," originally published in 1919 by Ezra Pound:

> The moment we use the copula, the moment we express subjective inclusions, poetry evaporates. The more concretely and vividly we express the interactions of things the better the poetry. We need in poetry thousands of active words, each doing its utmost to show forth the motive and vital forces. We can not exhibit the wealth of nature by mere summation, by the piling of sentences. Poetic thought works by suggestion, crowding maximum meaning into the single phrase, pregnant, charged, and luminous from within. (Fenollosa, 2008, p. 9)

Having some experience in poetic composition (Strate, 2015, 2020, 2023), I would note that it is actually much easier and much more common to leave out the verb *to be* in poetry than in prose. On the other hand, E-Prime would limit the use of metaphor, and figurative language is very much associated with creative writing. I would suggest that the technique of writing in E-Prime is useful in making authors more aware of their use of language, and the alternatives that they can consider. But I would not recommend it as a practice to be followed religiously for either creative or expository writing.

As difficult as it is to eliminate the copula completely in writing, how much more so would it be to speak in E-Prime? Most discussions of E-Prime seem to ignore the distinction between orality and literacy that is fundamental for the media ecology approach (Strate, 2017b). But at least one general semanticist, E. W. Kellogg III, reports that it is possible to learn how to speak in this way, starting with writing, and moving on to speech (Kellogg, 1987). Indeed, it is interesting to consider whether doing so would even be conceivable without first embracing E-Prime via the written word, and more generally whether literacy is a prerequisite for such a self-conscious approach to languaging. Without a doubt, it would require a great deal of practice and discipline to become fluent in E-Prime, and it is conceivable that there would be individuals who would accept the rigors necessary to gain such mastery. But it is hard to imagine widespread adoption of the practice.

I do want to make it clear that, while offering my own opinions, my intent here is not to provide a comprehensive summary of the debate over E-Prime, nor to provide a definitive statement refuting the proposal to eliminate the verb *to be* in its entirety. It seems to me that the critics of E-Prime question its viability as a solution that can be imposed on an entire population, or sold through a persuasive campaign, and question its effectiveness in achieving the goals established by Korzybski and his fellow general semanticists. For the most part, however, they view E-Prime as somewhat beneficial, and otherwise harmless, or mostly harmless. Contrary to that view, the respected linguistics scholar Robin T. Lakoff argues that "encouraging the replacement of *be* with other constructions will often have the effect of changing an illogical proposition from an assertion to a presupposition" (p. 144). To give an example that illustrates her point, take the following sentence: *Donald Trump is President of the United States and has dissolved the Attorney General's office on July 4th, 2022*. In this instance the *is* in the statement marks it as a proposition that can be evaluated and determined to be false (as he was no longer president in 2022). That false assertion is transformed into a presupposition via E-Prime as follows: *United States President Donald Trump has dissolved the Attorney General's office on July 4th, 2022*. The statement, "Donald Trump is President of the United States in 2022" is in a propositional form that allows for fact-checking, and therefore can be determined to be false to facts. The phrase "United States President Donald Trump in 2022" instead asserts that this is the case, that while the reality remains that he was no longer president at that time, insists that the reverse is true, presupposes rather than proposes.

Undoubtedly, there are undesirable effects associated with E-Prime, as there are with any innovation. For my part, I would say that one of the major drawbacks of eradicating the word *is* is that you would then be unable to say the phrase, *is not*, and therefore unable to say, *whatever you say it is, it isn't,* or *it is what it isn't*. The idea of non-identity that is foundational to general semantics is predicated on the pre-existing concept of identity. The goal is to move past identity relationships, not to forsake them altogether.

Zero-Copula Languages and the Orality-Literacy Factor

At this point, I would also note that while Korzybski was multilingual, he was not schooled in linguistics or philology, and the languages he learned were all from the Indo-European family, specifically his native Polish, Latin learned in school, French, and English, the language he wrote and taught in, for the most part. Indeed, he acknowledged that his recommendations regarding language reform were directed at the Indo-European languages. Neither were Bourland or Kellogg scholars with a background in the study of language. On the other hand, based on her expertise in linguistics, Lakoff (1992) notes,

> Modern Russian does not use *be* in the present tense at all. Most of the ancient Indo-European languages (for instance, Latin, Greek, and Sanskrit) could optionally omit *be* to create "nominal" sentences. There is, needless to say, very little evidence

indeed that speakers of these languages were any more logical than contemporary Americans. (p. 142)

The fact that Lakoff points to ancient languages should serve as a hint that orality-literacy studies would have something to contribute to our understanding of the role of the copula. And indeed it does. Eric Havelock (1978), in his brilliant work, *The Greek Concept of Justice*, devotes an entire chapter to "The Early History of the Verb 'to Be'". He begins the chapter by looking backwards from the literate philosophy of Plato to the nonliterate or oral poetry of Homer and Hesiod:

> The Platonic question Is justice truth? used to initiate the argument of the *Republic*, has a beguiling simplicity, concealing the fact that in order to use this kind of language certain logical (I prefer to say syntactical) requirements have to be met. Not only must both subject and predicate be completely stripped of personality and specificity, but the verb to be used to connect them must be invested with the function of denoting, not an act, or an event, but a relationship which is both logical and static, or, as Plato would say, "immovable." We have seen indications that neither the poetry of Homer nor that of Hesiod was capable of enunciating such a statement in its "Platonic" form, and this not just because it was poetry, but because it was oral poetry composed to meet the syntactical requirements of memorized speech. Hesiod can say what justice does, what is done to it, but not what it is. (p. 233)

Havelock (1978) acknowledges the fact that oral poetry is different from everyday speech, and that some may argue that the restrictions imposed by oral composition do not extend to ordinary discourse and therefore that the use of the copula by the ancient Greek in the street would be much like our own. While conceding that we can never determine the speech patterns of antiquity directly and definitively, Havelock notes that the metrical requirements of ancient Greek poetry in no way bar the poet from using the more abstract form of the verb *to be* that we are familiar with, suggesting that if it were in use in common speech it would have made its way into Homeric or Hesiodic diction. He goes on to argue that,

> It is true that the copula in modern vernaculars has become a routine method of indexing not merely rules and principles, like "Honesty is the best policy," but the "facts" of everyday life: "this house is large"; "the horse you sold me is lame"; "the corn is green"; "the Japanese are our enemies"; "he is very ill." Are we so sure that it was used in this routine way in archaic Greek speech? An acquaintance not only with nonepic poetry, but with the comedy and the prose of the high classical age, raises some doubts about this presumption. Would not such speech prefer idioms like: "this house looks-like large"; "the Japanese make war on us"; "he feels very ill" or "he ails"? This is not to deny that *einai* [to be] could be used with such simple subjects and predicates or some of them, but if used, would it not impart the notion of a presence "standing or looming in the distance" (in the case of the house), or "confronting us" (the Japanese)? The fact is that a vernacular tends to reflect the rules of syntax obeyed in preserved speech. Hence today, in order to speak "well," we speak a "literate" speech; under nonliterate conditions would one not have to obey "nonliterate" idiom in order to speak "well"? A member of a society restricted to oral communication would be more likely than his literate counterpart to invest his statements with a kind of dynamism. He would tend to perceive his environment not as a series of objects placed in relation to each other, but as a series of activities and processes in which objects play roles. His own experience of such would modulate itself in a series of actions and reactions to such activities. (pp. 247–248)

Havelock's argument, for which he provides numerous examples from ancient Greek texts extending over the half millennium that separates

Homer from Plato, is that the Greek language was characterized by an evolutionary development associated with literacy, moving from the relatively concrete to increasing levels of abstraction, and from a restricted use of the copula to one that resembles contemporary usage:

> Gradually, if sparingly, the verb "to be" appears as the copula required for a stated historical "fact" replacing the powerful and mobile "presence" assigned to the personalities of oral narrative. The phrase *potamos megas*—"river big"—expresses an oral vision (and incidentally constitutes a fragment of a hexameter). But *Olenos potamos megas esti*—Olenos is a big river" (Herodotus)—converts the vision into the likeness of an objective statement (though the preferred predicate is still a symbol of status). (Havelock, 1986, p. 110)

Havelock's focus is on ancient Greece, but his research serves as the basis for generalizations about the evolution of the copula in response to the introduction of the written word and the development of literate cultures. It suggests that the most problematic aspects of the verb *to be* and the *is* of identity are a result of this evolution, part of the cost we pay for all of the advantages that reading and writing bestow upon us. With this in mind, I would like to return to Robin Lakoff's point that there are languages that lack the verb *to be*, and in particular omit the verb in the present tense. It is perhaps more than coincidental that Korzybski refers to the *is* of the identity, not the *was* of identity or the *will be* of identity. No doubt he was aware of this fact, considering that for the first few decades of his life, his native Poland was part of the Russian empire, and he served in the Czar's army during the First World War, until he was wounded in battle and was sent to North America to lead a fundraising effort. Perhaps his awareness of this distinctive characteristic of the Russian language influenced him, at least in part, in his advice to avoid certain forms of the copula.

The linguistic phenomenon of *zero copula* appears across a wide range of languages, and in different variations. It is also characteristic of an African-American dialect of English, hence sentences such as, *You bad! She fine! Where he at?* This in turn has been the subject of widespread adoption in recent years, so that it is now quite commonplace to ask, *you ok?* or *you good?* It is also found in certain stand alone phrases like, *the sooner the better, the more the merrier, no pain no gain,* as well as, *the harder they come, the harder they fall.* These correlative expressions would not be classified as complete sentences by traditional, prescriptivist standards, but otherwise function as such and therefore would be understood as sentences from a descriptivist perspective. The point here is that even for languages that fully embrace the *is* of identity, we can find instances in which the verb *to be* is omitted, a fact that should provide some comfort to E-Prime enthusiasts.

But I want to return to the specific phenomenon of languages lacking the present tense form of the verb *to be*. Another language that does not have words corresponding to *is*, *are*, or *am* is Hebrew. And, to return to a phrase I mentioned earlier, translations of

אֶהְיֶה אֲשֶׁר אֶהְיֶה

to mean *I am Who I am* are considered erroneous in Jewish tradition precisely because Hebrew has no present tense form of the verb *to be*, and this in turn is why *I will be what I will be* is the preferred translation. Having gone to Hebrew School when I was young, what I was told was the present tense of the verb *to be* was not used, but was understood; this would be similar to the way that the subject of the sentence is understood in commands like, *Come here! Stand up!* and *Go away!* And it was certainly how I understood it, and I would imagine that anyone learning Hebrew as a second language understood it in that way as well. I would further suggest that native Hebrew speakers do so too, supporting Lakoff's contention that they are not significantly more logical or non-aristotelian than native English speakers, and I would also suggest that the fact that that population would be almost entirely literate would be at least a contributing factor. I do want to consider, however, the implications of this form of zero copula.

Tense Disagreement

We think of verb conjugation as involving three basic tenses, past, present and future. Of course, in actuality there are quite a few more, simple present and present perfect, and corresponding versions for the past and future, present progressive and past progressive, present continuous and the past and future versions, present perfect continuous and the past and future versions, and modals and all of the different forms of the conditionals and subjunctives. But the three main tenses correspond to our conception of time as divided into past, present, and future. We take this for granted as if our way of representing time is a faithful reflection of time itself, but we have long since learned that, while widely held, it is not universal to our species, or to our languages. This was one of the main findings that Benjamin Lee Whorf (1956) took away from his research on the languages of the Hopi and Navajo. It is also the case that the standard view of past, present, and future was challenged by Einstein's revolution in physics, and it is worth noting that Korzybski was inspired by Einstein's non-newtonian physics and non-euclidean geometry to devise his non-aristotelian system of thought. Indeed, Einstein's theory of relativity suggests that time does not exist as a separate phenomenon, that it only exists as part of the unified phenomenon of spacetime, and that all of time exists at once, even though we can only perceive part of it; it is not the case that the past disappears and the future has not come into being yet, but rather that it is all present at once. Depending on our own position and velocity in space relative to others, time may appear to progress faster or more slowly for us, and events may be perceived in different sequence.

I do question Einstein's view that time is an illusion and nothing more than another spatial dimension (I believe that the reverse may be true), but from the point of view of physics, the concept of *now* is impossible to define, which also means that it is impossible to determine whether two events occurring in different locations are simultaneous or not. And simply to determine what *now* means, we have to be able to say at what point does the present become the past. We can suggest answers based on human psychology and neurological activity, looking to the way that memory works for example, but there is no objective measure of what *now* means, and what we consider to be immediate is still subject to the lag time, however miniscule, between the event, the reception of data about the event via sense perception, and the processing of it via our nervous systems and brain. Tom Wolfe (1968) brings this up in *The Electric Kool-Aid Acid Test*, his report on Ken Kesey and the Merry Pranksters back in the 60s, and how Neal Cassady tried to get as close as possible to the actual event through the use of amphetamines:

> A person has all sorts of lags built into him, Kesey is saying. One, the most basic, is the sensory lag, the lag between the time your senses receive something and you are able to react. One-thirtieth of a second is the time it takes, if you're the most alert person alive, and most people are a lot slower than that. Now Cassady is right up against that 1/30th of a second barrier. He is going as fast as a human can go, but even he can't overcome it. He is a living example of how close you can come, but it can't be done. You can't go any faster than that. You can't through sheer speed overcome the lag. We are all of us doomed to spend the rest of our lives watching a *movie* of our lives—we are always acting on what has just finished happening. It happened at least 1/30th of a second ago. We think we're in the present, but we aren't. The present we know is only a movie of the past, and we will really never be able to control the present through ordinary means. That lag has to be overcome some other way, through some kind of total breakthrough. (p. 144)

By way of contrast, St. Augustine in his *Confessions* (Book 11, 20:26) grapples with the three tenses of past, present, and future, and concludes that only the present exists, at least as far as we are concerned:

> What is by now evident and clear is, that neither future nor past exists, and it is inexact language to speak of three times—past, present and future. Perhaps it would be exact to say: there are three times, a present of things past, a present of things present, a present of things to come. In the soul there are these three aspects of time, and I do not see them anywhere else. The present considering the past is memory, the present considering the present is immediate awareness, the present considering the future is expectation. If we are allowed to use such language, I see three times, and I admit they are three. Moreover, we may say, There are three times, past, present, and future. This customary way of speaking is incorrect, but it is common usage. Let us accept the usage. I do not object and offer no opposition or criticism, as long as what is said is being understood, namely that neither the future nor the past is now present. There are few usages of everyday speech which are exact, and most of our language is inexact. Yet what we mean is communicated. (1991, p. 235)

While this view may seem self-evident, it can alternately be understood as the product of language and culture as, for example, Whorf's (1956) somewhat controversial findings provide an alternative conceptualization; he explains that the Hopi do not have a concept of tense as we understand it, instead referring to events as existing or not existing, manifest or unmanifest; manifest incorporates both the present and the past, as both are real in an objective sense, while unmanifest incorporates the future and the conditional, both not yet real although existing in potential (see also Nystrom, 2021).

What Einstein, Wolfe, Augustine, and Whorf all have in common is that they point to the uncertainty regarding the temporal concept of the present, and its corresponding linguistic representation as the present tense. With this in mind, the idea of languages that omit the present tense of the verb *to be*, while alien to speakers of English (and many other languages), ought to seem less radical a departure than it might have otherwise. And it may perhaps seem more easily justifiable as an alternative to more copular types of language, albeit not having achieved this form of zero copula in the conscious manner of E-Prime users. In demonstrating that the present tense copula is optional, perhaps even unnecessary, they isolate the words *is*, *are*, and *am* as the main troublemakers leading to Korzybski's critique of the *is of identity* and the *is of predication*. Further incorporating Havelock's (1978, 1986) discussion of how those words can change as we move from language based on the requirements of oral communication and oral tradition, to language altered by the addition of systems of writing and habits of literacy is especially helpful now.

What does it mean to use the word *is* in the present tense? If I say that, *the sky is blue*, do I mean that it is blue today? Blue right now? Or do I mean that *blue* is an inherent characteristic of the sky? That it is a permanent feature, immovable to use Plato's term? That it is *always-already* blue? That it is *now-and-forever* blue? Contrast this with the statement, *the sky is gray*. In this instance, we understand that the *is* in that statement refers to a present time that is transitory and ephemeral, that it refers to some sense of the idea of now. *The sky is gray* can only make sense as a statement belonging to a specific period of time, a statement that is inherently subject to change, whereas *the sky is blue* can be understood as a timeless statement, a statement that invokes a sense of permanence. Paul Watzlawick and his colleagues note that the concept of permanence became fully realized in Plato's philosophy, derived from pre-Socratic speculation about the nature of reality on the part of the Ionian physicists, who first posited the idea of indivisible building blocks referred to as atoms (Watzlawick, Weakland, & Fisch, 1974). This evolution follows the same path that Havelock laid out as the transition from orality to literacy in ancient Greece. One connection would be the fact that permanence is a highly abstract concept, and literacy is associated with a greater potential for abstract thinking and expression, whereas orality is associated with relatively concrete modes of thought and communication. As previously noted, in the oral tradition that produced the Homeric epics, there is no abstract notion of justice, such as appears in Plato's dialogues; instead, justice is a characteristic grounded in specific actions performed by specific actors (e.g., gods and heroes).

In addition to the abstract quality of permanence, there is the sense of fixity tied to the written word, in contrast to the ephemeral nature of speech. As Walter Ong (1982) puts it, "sound exists only when it is going out of existence" (p. 32). Oral poetry gives us winged words, language in motion, fleeting, impossible to freeze. Writing fixes words in place, transforms language from an event, a happening, to a thing, something to have and to hold, from this time forth and forever, something set in stone and unmovable. We might therefore discern some earlier hints of the concept of permanence in the religious thought of the first alphabetic culture of ancient Israel, and to a lesser degree in the ancient civilizations of Egypt and Mesopotamia. But the radical shift that takes place in ancient Greece that results in the concept of permanence that we take for granted is inextricably linked to the changes in language and thought brought on by the introduction of the Greek alphabet, and this includes the changes that were made to the copula.

For literates such as ourselves, the oral mindset appears quite alien, more so than many depictions of extraterrestrials in science fiction narratives. It is challenging to empathize with this sort of way of looking at the world, but scholars such as Havelock and Ong were able to do so. Let us therefore try to imagine a worldview in which the concept of permanence is absent. Such a worldview would be consistent with the language of the Hopi as discussed by Whorf (1956), in which phenomena tend to be referred to as *events* rather than *things*. *Events*, happenings, come into being and then, *event*ually, disappear. They are defined by their temporal limitations. *Things* are clearly not necessarily characterized by permanence, not for us, not for Plato, and as previously noted, physics tells us that nothing is permanent, that all phenomena are events in spacetime, and all matter is composed of energy. But referring to phenomena as *things* opens the door to the illusion of permanence, and the difference between the noun-based European languages and the verb-based Hopi and Navajo languages that Whorf identifies is also the difference between languages that have been modified by centuries of literacy, and languages that have not been mutated in this way.

Changing Conceptions of Time

The shift from active to static language is linked to changing conceptions of time in a number of ways. For example, writing is associated with linearity, including a linear notion of time, taking the form of chronology and history. This stands in contrast to the cyclical notion of time associated with oral cultures, and with the observance of natural phenomena, the cycles of day and night, the waning and waxing of the moon, the ebb and flow of tides, the coming and going of the seasons. This is also the way of the nomadic society, not aimless wanderings, but circuits repeated again and again. A cyclical view of time recognizes the rhythms of the external world, and our own internal ones, and therefore the constancy of change. This view also places special emphasis on what we call the past, the point of origin, the moment of birth, the return to where it all began. There is the desire to *get back to the garden*, to return to Eden, to recapture the Golden Age, to enter the aboriginal Dreamtime. Ritual provides a means of entering this mythic time, reenactment of events linked to the moment of creation or foundation is a way to reconnect with it, and even more, to enter into it. Mircea Eliade (1954, 1959) explained that this myth of eternal return is not about travelling back in historical time, as if by time machine, but by entering into a different dimension of time, a sacred time that is separate and distinct from the everyday, profane time that we inhabit. Being outside of profane time, sacred time is neither past, present, or future in a linear sense, but one that intersects, or can be accessed, from any moment in profane time. While situated in the past from the profane point of view, it is also timeless and eternal. The idea of permanence refers to an unchanging state within profane time, whereas the creative era or moment of origination of sacred time is an event that is continually happening, always unfolding.

Literacy does not automatically negate the experience of sacred time, but writing does open the door to linear time, chronology and history, and the idea of progress. This ultimately turns our attention away from the past and the desire to return to or recapture a golden age, and leads us to look towards the future, towards things getting better and better, to progress, finally leading to utopia (Strate, 2011b). The present is no longer a faded shadow of the past, a decadent time, but rather the best of times so far, and a point along a continuum leading to continual improvement. Through writing and related devices, first the calendar and later the mechanical clock, our sense of time becomes homogenized. Days and years are treated as equal and interchangeable units, as are hours, minutes, seconds, etc. Edward T. Hall (1983) refers to cultures that adopt this view as *monochronic*, as opposed to *polychronic* cultures that allow for different kinds of time, most notably the sacred as well as the profane. William Blake tried to recapture the long lost worldview of sacred time and space in his "Auguries of Innocence", writing that you can, "see a World in a Grain of Sand, and a Heaven in a Wild Flower, Hold Infinity in the Palm of your hand, And Eternity in an hour," but he still had to do so by reference to the profane clock time of the hour, and an earthly sense of place. As the product of the literate and typographic culture of 17th century England, his sensibility was very much influenced by the ideal of permanence. In this context, heaven becomes, to invoke the lyrics of the song by Talking Heads, *a place where nothing ever happens*.

Conclusion

I have previously argued that whereas the shift from orality to literacy is associated with a shift from an orientation that looks to the past to one that looks to the future, the more recent shift to an electronic media environment is associated with an orientation entirely centered on the present (Strate, 2011b). This is based on the instantaneity and immediacy of electronic transmission; the ability of audiovisual recording, especially as further amplified by digital technology, to recreate the past in the present; and the use of computer technologies to program the future, thereby bringing it into the present. This represents permanence taken to its extreme.

If we imagine, instead, the complete absence of the idea of permanence, then the concept of the present is reduced nearly to the point of insignificance. I have earlier noted that from the point of view of physics, the concept of *now* is difficult if not impossible to nail down. If we allow for a less precise, more human interpretation of the present as based on the experience of the moment, this ephemeral, transitory time still pales in comparison with the enormity of all that constitutes the past. And of all that will occur in the future. Indeed, we arrive at a viewpoint diametrically opposed to Augustine, one in which the present does not really exist. Rather, drawing on Ken Kesey, we have the most recent past, as recent as 1/30th of a second ago, perception being always in the past, but even our conscious awareness lagging behind the firing of the nerve cells of the brain that serve as the basis of our thought. And we have our predictions, expectations, anticipations of the future, again even to a fraction of a second, based on what our minds are processing. In this sense, the future passes almost immediately into the past, but even allowing for a sense of the present that extends a bit further, its scope is by its very nature limited. Now, imagine the language that goes with or perhaps conveys this sense of time, a sense of time in which events occur, coming into being and then disappearing. Imagine a language in which the *is* of permanence is absent, that only employs the *is* of momentary events. In such a language, the importance of the verb *to be* would be significantly reduced compared to, say, modern English. It might even be possible to do without the present tense of the verb, without the *is*, *am*, and *are* that we rely on. In this way, we can understand how there might be such zero copula languages, although this form of *copula-shun* would not prevent them from adopting literate conceptions of identity and permanence.

For languages such as English that have the present tense of the verb *to be*, and have been modified by literacy, the difficulty lies with the fact that we are dealing with two very similar meanings of the word *is*; two meanings that are similar yes, and yet that slight, generally overlooked distinction between the two connotations is a difference that makes a difference, and indeed it is no small one. And it is one that we are prone to confuse. For example, does the statement, *Donald is a criminal*, refer to a distinct period of time, or a permanent, immutable characteristic of the individual? Does the statement, *Donald is President of the United States*, imply that this is true for a limited term, or is it permanently so? As noted, Korzybski offered several extensional devices for countering various problems caused by an Aristotelian logic, among them dating, adding dates to clarify such statements. We could, for example, add the years 2017–2021 to the statement, *Donald is President of the United States*, to make that statement more precise. This works for statements in which it is possible to determine a specific set of dates or years, and we can otherwise use the device of qualifying terms to say, for example, that the sky is overcast *today*, or *this morning*.

Robert Heinlein in his influential science fiction novel, *Stranger in a Strange Land*, introduced a future occupation called a *fair witness*, someone trained in general semantics to never make an inference. As he explained it, if you were to point at a house at some distance away, and ask a fair witness what color it is, that person would answer, *it is white, on this side* (because the other side would not be visible to the fair witness). What he neglected to include was, *it is white, on this side, at this moment*; that the time period was omitted comes as no great surprise, but rather represents a reflection of how difficult it is for us to eliminate the *is* of permanence. And we could add to the qualifying terms, saying, I *perceive the house to be white on this side at this time*, or to be even more specific and attach a specific date and time to the statement, but at this point we run the risk of annoying others in our everyday interactions. Put another way, to be overly precise and overly qualifying in the wrong context would be a form of stupid talk, or in some contexts an effort at evasion (as in testimony under oath where a statement accompanied by "to the best of my recollection" can immunize the speaker from being accused of perjury for stating a falsehood or avoiding giving an answer). It can also bog the communication down to the point that it becomes dysfunctional. Relational considerations are essential, because they are the basis of how we make meaning, interpret messages, and evaluate them. Korzybski's devices are a useful educational tool, but not a practical solution to the overall problem. The same might be said of E-Prime, and the discussion here might suggest a modified form of E-Prime, call it *E-Prime-Prime* if you like, in which only the present tense of the verb *to be* is eliminated. But again, many uses of *is*, *am*, and *are* were not considered a problem by Korzybski. His primary concern was with identity, and within that I believe that the primary concern regarding identity has to do with permanence.

The problem with the saying, *it is what it is*, I would conclude, has much to do with concept of permanence, not so much that something is identical to itself, but that it is not subject to change. Even if identity is an illusion, it is a useful one, allowing us to make generalizations about the world. What we need to do is to internalize the idea that all of our statements are tentative, that all of our maps are subject to change, because they are incomplete and because the territory itself is changing. Various devices and techniques can help, changing the way we use language can help, but ultimately it requires awareness on our part, a new kind of consciousness. Consciousness of abstracting. Consciousness of structures and relations. Consciousness of time. One hundred years ago, Korzybski (1921) started down this path by writing a book on time-binding. We still have a long way to go.

Figments of a Fragment, or Fragments of a **Figment**

Chapter 4

Imagination is our only reality. Which is to say that what we call our reality is in fact imagined. What we call our environment is composed of events in spacetime, events in timespace, happenings that only exist as they are going out of existence. They cannot be captured or held. They cannot be fixed or frozen. They cannot be known directly and immediately.

The events that make up our environment are fleeting and fugitive, elusive and evasive, oblique and mysterious. Our access to whatever is going on out there is terribly limited and entirely indirect, and as a consequence, we have no choice but to make things up as we go along.

The reality we think that we inhabit is an imagined reality. We are all citizens of an imagined country, members of an imagined community. Imagination is an environment that surrounds us, that we live and love and work and play within. Where there is life, there is imagination. Where there is imagination, there is no exit, as long as there is life.

Imagination is an environment, and an environment is composed of events. Therefore, imagination too is made up of events. Imagination, it follows, is not a thing. It is not something we have, or that we lack. Imagination is something that we do. Like thinking. Or breathing.

There is no such *thing* as imagination. There is only *imagining*. A verb, rather than a noun. An action and activity. An act that we perform, a performance that we conduct, often for an audience of one, one's own self. But we can also imagine together, and share our imaginings with others.

Imagination is an event. Imagination may be said to occur only within a mind, within some form of consciousness. But it may well be that it is through a set of acts of imagination that mind and consciousness come into existence, that they emerge out of a collective series of imaginings.

A book, a play, a poem, a film, a story, a drawing, a painting, a piece of music, etc., may be *products* of imagination, but the products are not imagination itself. They are the effects, not the cause.

Imagination begins with memory. Indeed, memory constitutes a primal form of imagination. To remember is to imagine. When we remember, we do not playback a recording, we *call* something up, we *recall* something, something summoned up out of the depths. We imagine, or rather re-imagine, what we once experienced. What we imagine we experienced is not the same experience as what we experienced in the past. Neither is it the same experience when we remember repeatedly. Each remembering is a new experience, a new act of imagining.

The imagined past may be more or less faithful to what actually occurred, but it is never identical to it. Memory is a map of a territory that is no longer available to us. A map of an imagined territory. A map of a map. We imagine our own imaginings.

Experience based on sense perception is more than the passive reception of information from outside of ourselves. It is the active processing of the sensory data that we take in, the filtering and organizing and interpreting of sensory data. It is the making of meaning. This too is a primal form of imagination. As the saying goes, *we see things not as they are, but as we are.*

Sensory data is a response to stimuli that are nothing more than irritations of our nervous systems. Irritations that cause nerve cells to fire in varying sequences and combinations, until they reach the brain where the data is processed. Until they reach the mind, where we make sense of what our senses convey to us. The making of meaning out of the irritation of nerve endings and the resulting cascade of signals they produce is a pure act of imagination. Our meaning making may be of a modest sort, as when we recognize a familiar face or place. Or it may be a grand form of imagining, as when we interpret natural events as omens and portents, or use them to generate theories and hypotheses. Moreover, the sensory data that we imagine with may be generated from within, as when we hear voices and see visions, or feel a phantom pain, or when we are asleep and dreaming.

We imagine when we remember what we once experienced, and that enables us to imagine past events that we never experienced for ourselves. Experience and memory also allow us to imagine events that have yet to occur. Events that will be and events that may be. Events that could be and events that should be. We can imagine how events that occurred in the past might repeat themselves in the future. We can imagine past events that never actually occurred, and predict, project, and plan for future events that never happened before. The failure to anticipate unprecedented events is often referred to as a *failure of imagination.*

At its best, the act of imagination is a creative act, resulting in works of art. Innovations and inventions. Enhanced understanding and enlightenment. Progress. Making things better. Repairing the world. Improving the environment. Building new realities. Utopia.

At its worst, the act of imagination is a destructive act. The imagination of disaster. Substituting illusions for ideals. Delusions for dreams. Acts that cause damage and harm. The ushering in of the fall. The creation of catastrophe.

Imagination is an environment. Experience and memory are contained within my imagination. I can be lost in my imagination. I can be found in my imagination. I retreat to my imagination for safety and comfort. At once a humble home, and a theatre where I am both audience and actor, as well as a palace of magnificent proportions, my imagination is a construction that can be expanded and enriched. My imagination is not limited to my own thoughts, or contained within my own mind, but extends beyond me to regions that are shared with others, through acts of collaboration, through our collective imagining.

We imagine. We imagine our reality. We imagine ourselves. We imagine ourselves imagining. Remembering, we imagine ourselves imagining in the past. Self-consciously, we imagine ourselves imagining in the present. Speculatively, we imagine ourselves imagining in the future.

Imagination is only what we imagine it to be.

Imagination is only a figment.

&c

Part 3

So You Want to Change the World? A Hitchhiker's Guide to **Subversive Thinking**

My title begins with a question, *so you want to change the world?* I suppose you might consider it presumptuous of me to assume that you do in fact want to change the world. After all, one of the basic rules in general semantics is to avoid making assumptions, because we all know what happens when you assume (on the off chance you are not familiar with the saying, which functions as a mnemonic to aid in remembering how to spell the word, as well as a caution against confusing inferences with facts, it goes like this: "When you *assume*, you make an *ass* out of you (*u*) and *me*"). So, I plead guilty of violating this rule, but I do so with an explanation.

First, however, let me concede that some of you may not be interested in changing the world. Given the state of the economy, some of you may only be concerned with supporting yourselves financially, making a living, getting and keeping a job. If that is the case, then you may want to stop reading right now. But if you decide to continue, I think you may still find something useful in what I'm going to discuss here.

But I suspect that most of you want something more out of life than just a paycheck, despite the fact that times are tough. Back in the sixties, Marshall McLuhan (1964; McLuhan & Fiore, 1967) observed that while the baby boomers' parents, the folks we now call the greatest generation, were content to have *jobs*, their children wanted something more: They wanted *roles*. Now, the experience of the greatest generation was certainly colored by the Great Depression, a time when finding any kind of employment was cause for celebration, and you did what you had to do to try make ends meet. Your life was not your work.

Work was a necessity of life, something you did in order to be able to live your life. Your job was kept separate and compartmentalized from the rest of your life, from your real life, which included family and friends, community and religion, music and dancing, games and sports, theatre and movies, and reading for pleasure.

By way of contrast, the baby boomers said they wanted something more than just a job. Often the refrain would be, I want to do something meaningful, something relevant, something creative. Or, I want to do something I love. Or, in its most prosaic sense, it was, I don't just want a job, I want a career. In other words, for the baby boomers and the generations that followed them, work was no longer seen as something apart from life. Instead, work became an integral part of life, and for some the most important part of their lives. When McLuhan said that young people want roles instead of jobs, he meant that finding their life's work was a vital part of their journey of self-discovery, their search for identity, their quest to find out who they really are. A job is something you *do*, a role is something you *are*. It is a sense of self, a *self* that you put on, that you become (Goffman, 1959; see also Strate, 2022). Of course, when so much of our sense of self becomes bound up with our employment, losing your job results in not just financial hardship, but an identity crisis.

You may recall the lines from the Broadway musical that debuted during the 1970s, *A Chorus Line*: "I really need this job. Please God I need this job. I've got to get this job." The job in question is a role in a play, and it is worthwhile to understand that we also play different roles in life, the role of child and for many of us, the role of parent; the role of student, and sometimes the role of teacher; the role of friend, of lover, of spouse, of colleague. Every role we play is a different, individual self in its own right, and each one of us is the sum of all the different roles we play, the sum of the different selves that we accumulate (Goffman, 1959). Some roles may be more important than others, and sometimes we may fall in love with a role so deeply that we wind up playing it all the time, no matter what the situation. But in truth, different situations call on us to play different roles, and the roles that we play are defined by our relationships with others. Parents are the product of their children, teachers are the product of their students, leaders are made by their followers. As Gregory Bateson (1972, 1979) explained, a role is only half of a relationship. And we are much better off when our approach to the roles that we play is flexible, rather than being rigidly fixated on any one role, any one sense of self, any one way of defining ourselves. There are always alternatives, always new facets of our identities to explore and develop, new roles that we can play. The roles you play, the selves you become, are your greatest art forms, your most creative achievements.

On the surface, it may seem like the differences between jobs and roles can be boiled down to the difference between the depression-era mentality of the greatest generation and the affluence that accompanied the postwar baby boom. But I suspect that, for the most part, Generation X, Generation Y or the Millennials, and Generation Z all share the same view as the boomers (Twenge, 2023), as will the up and coming Generation Alpha. And I know that the greatest generation did not invent their view of what work is all about, but inherited it from the generations that came before, many of them benefiting from times of economic boom. So, rather than economics, we can instead look to the early 20th century invention of the assembly line as the most extreme manifestation of the idea of the factory job. And we can look further back to the idea of division of labor that informed the 19th century industrial revolution, fueled by the innovation of the steam engine, which also gave birth to the approach known as scientific management, with its emphasis on efficiency above all else (Ellul, 1964; Postman, 1992). But McLuhan (1962, 1964) would have us trace the origins of this mentality further back, to the printing revolution initiated by Johann Gutenberg in the 15th century. The printing press represented the first mechanization of a handicraft, and opened the door to a revolution in mechanization both by way of example and by initiating a knowledge explosion that continues to this day. Printing especially encouraged specialization and fragmentation, traits intrinsic to mechanical devices, to factories and assembly lines, and to the idea of work as separate from life. In fact, apart from the making of books, printers also engaged in what was referred to as *job printing*, the printing of catalogues, calendars, posters, and of no small significance, the printing of blank forms, the foundation of bureaucratic organization in government and business (Eisenstein, 1979; Steinberg, 1996). This is the origin of the word *job*, which at first only referred to a "piece of work," a specific task to be performed, a bit of work for a hired hand. It wasn't until the 17th century that it evolved to mean more generally, "work done for pay."

The printing revolution was the turning point, but McLuhan (1962, 1964) would remind us that the seeds were sown much earlier, with the invention of the alphabet, which takes us back to almost 4,000 years ago, and we can push the date back even further to the development of the first writing system some 5,500 years ago (Goody, 1977). The first signs of specialization and fragmentation can be seen within the literate cultures of the ancient world, but their full potential was not unlocked until the advent of typography.

Along the same lines, the seeds of our new way of looking at the world were sown in the 19th century with the invention of the telegraph, the telephone, and the wireless, the first form of radio, not to mention the electric light. Electric technology and electronic communications gave rise to new ways of thinking about the world, which took the form of Einstein's theory of relativity and Heisenberg's uncertainty principle in science, Picasso's cubism and the modern art movement along with its postmodern successors in art, and Claude Shannon's information theory, Norbert Wiener's cybernetics, and Alan Turing's universal machine, all of which form the basis of the modern computer and information technology. The potential of the electronic media began to be fully realized with the introduction of television, which became the dominant medium of communication in the postwar period. Growing up with television is the single defining characteristic that set baby boomers apart from the generations that came before, opening up what came to be known as the generation gap, a generation gap unlike any present-day divide between the so-called digital natives and digital immigrants. The turmoil of the sixties had much to do with the disruptive impact of the television medium. And while electronic media have continued to evolve towards their full potential with the addition of the internet, the web, social media, mobile technologies, AI, etc., for the past seven decades we have moved increasingly further into a new form of post-literate, post-typographic, post-mechanical, post-industrial, electronic culture. We live in what McLuhan (1962, 1964) calls a *global village*, and through electronic communications we can feel like we ourselves have the whole world in our hands. And given the way things are today, as much as we have made enormous progress in so many ways over the past century, it is only natural to want to change the world, to make things better.

Speaking of jobs and computers brings to mind the famous quote from the founder of Apple, Inc., Steve Jobs, back in the early eighties. He was recruiting John Sculley, then president of Pepsi-Cola, to come aboard as CEO of Apple, and he said to him: *Do you want to sell sugared water for the rest of your life? Or do you want to come with me and change the world?* Sculley took over the reins of Apple in 1983, and the following year Jobs introduced the Macintosh, which truly did change the world. A year after that, Sculley forced Jobs to leave Apple, and Sculley's leadership eventually brought the company to the brink of bankruptcy, until he was forced out after a decade at the helm; Sculley's departure paved the way for Jobs to return in 1997 and turn the company into the behemoth it is today. And the question that Steve Jobs posed to John Sculley is essentially the question of whether you want to remain in a career that is little more than a job, or do you want to take on a role with all the world as your stage? For Jobs and Sculley, it was a genuine question. As it appears in the title of my talk, the question may seem rhetorical. But given the way things worked out with Sculley, it's tempting to say, *So you want to change the world? Don't!*

Of course, if I really meant it, I wouldn't have much of a talk. So I hasten to add that I say *don't* not to discourage, but to caution. We know that all too often attempts to change the world for the better have led to disaster. Whatever the benefits may be from the changes we make, there will always be a cost that accompanies them, and only a fool makes a purchase without looking at the price tag. And whatever the expected outcome of the changes we bring about, there will always be additional consequences that we did not, and could not anticipate. And the changes that are introduced will lead to other changes, and those to still other changes, as the direct effects lead to indirect effects, effects of effects, and effects of effects of effects, and so on (for more on this and the discussion of effects that follows, see Strate, 2014, 2017a, 2017b).

Changes

A philosophy professor used to pose the following scenario to his class. Suppose some kind of space god from another world came down here to the United States, and told the American people that he would give us a great gift that would vastly increase our mobility and freedom. And all he would ask in return, given that he is an old-fashioned kind of god, would be for us to sacrifice some thirty to forty thousand American lives to him each year. Now, would anyone in his right mind say yes, this is a good deal? But this is exactly the deal we made to the great god of technology in adopting the automobile and making it a central feature of our society. This change has had many unintended, unanticipated effects, some of them negative, some not. For example, the automobile was invented so that we could go from point A to point B faster than before, but no one anticipated that this would lead us to move farther away from where we work, and spend more time commuting back and forth, leading to the enormous growth of the suburbs. Neither did anyone foresee that the automobile would result in our paving over a large part of our country, and cause us to become dependent on petroleum, influencing our foreign policy in significant ways. Nor did anyone consider how the automobile would liberate young people, changing mating habits, so that a generation of Americans would be conceived in the backseats of their grandparents' station wagons. No one expected the automobile to empower minorities, for example by placing African-Americans on an equal footing with whites, which helped to create the foundation for the Civil Rights movement. And no one expected the automobile to empower women to a very significant degree as well. Think about soccer moms and their SUVs, for example, as well as the prohibition in effect until recently in Saudi Arabia.

When changes are introduced, there will always be negative effects that cannot be separated from the positive ones, just as every pharmaceutical has its side effects, and the key is to try to make sure the side effects are minimized. And there will always be unintended and unanticipated effects along with the effects that are intended and anticipated. And whatever the direct effects may be, there will always be indirect effects resulting from them. And the point here is that we need to approach change carefully, not in a blind rush towards the next big thing. Again, I am not denying the need for change. I firmly believe that our purpose in life is what in the Kabbalah is referred to as *tikkun olam*, the healing of the world. And in the spirit of healing, we might follow the advice often attributed to the Hippocratic Oath, *first, do no harm*. And there are times as well when the New Testament proverb, *physician, heal thyself*, best sums up what is needed, or as Mahatma Gandhi put it, *Be the change that you wish to see in the world*. The important point is that change comes in many different varieties. You can change your outlook, your mindset, your worldview, your consciousness. You can change your patterns of behavior, your relationships, your situation in life. You can change your environment, and change the other people in your environment. There are changes you can make within the system you are working in, and some of those changes may only result in maintaining the status quo, in homeostasis. And there are changes you can make to the system itself, and they represent the most radical kind of change. For any initiative, in order to maximize the benefits, and minimize the costs, we have to determine what kind of change is needed. And that means we have to determine what are the problems we are trying to solve and what are the goals we are trying to achieve. And then, what are the concrete steps we need to take to achieve those goals (Johnson, 1946).

What I am talking about, then, is neither resisting change nor engaging in change for the sake of change, but rather a thoughtful, reflective approach to change, whether it's changing *the* world, or just changing *your* world. The great anthropologist Margaret Mead once said, *Never doubt that a small group of thoughtful, committed, citizens can change the world. Indeed, it is the only thing that ever has*. And I want to underline the fact that she referred to a group of people, and not an isolated individual. Steve Jobs didn't start Apple by himself, and he didn't make it a success all by himself. Working together, we arrive at more and better solutions that working alone. I also want to invoke a saying that has its origins with the Scottish biologist, sociologist, and pioneer of urban studies, Patrick Geddes: *Think globally, act locally*. This saying reminds us to pay attention to the concrete reality that is right in front of our eyes, rather than get lost in vague abstractions. It reminds us to keep our focus on the human lifeworld, and keep in mind the importance of community.

Hitching a Ride

So you want to change the world? What I have to offer you is not a blueprint or recipe or formula, which is why I decided to call it a hitchhiker's guide. And that of course is an homage to the humorist Douglas Adams, and his *Hitchhiker's Guide to the Galaxy*. That novel and its sequels are not only humorous, but comedies in the classic sense, which means stories of survival. Comic heroes are ordinary individuals much like ourselves, or even of lesser power and ability than ourselves, who just try to get by in an often hostile environment. By way of contrast, tragic heroes are persons of superior status and ability who try to take control of their environment, and in doing so, end up bringing about their own doom. Tragedy, then, is a story about blowback, about an individual vying for control against a hostile environment, and trying to change the world in a way that backfires (Meeker, 1997). And it is a type of plotline that is closely associated with literacy and print culture, with its centered subjectivity or sense of self (Strate, 2022). Comedy, on the other, represents an ecological view of the world, about someone who is just trying to live in harmony with the environment (Meeker, 1997), and it is the dominant mode of narrative in nonliterate, oral cultures, and again now in our postliterate, electronic culture.

The role of the hitchhiker fits in perfectly with the concept of comedy, as someone who is not in the driver's seat, who is not trying to take total control of the environment, someone who must depend on the kindness of strangers, get along with and work together with others, someone who has to think locally, conserve resources, and yet, still, someone who is able to effect change by finding a way to travel from one place to another, to reach a desired destination. And in this sense, we are all hitchhikers travelling along roads we never made, through environments we did not create and only were born into, depending on tools, machines, and methods most of which were developed by people who long ago passed away, and expressing ourselves through words and symbols that we did not invent. And yet, in hitching a ride, there exists the possibility of progress, both individually and collectively.

So I offer this as a hitchhikers guide to subversive thinking, and I use the word subversive here as a nod to the work of my mentor, Neil Postman, and one of his best known works, a book co-authored by Charles Weingartner entitled, *Teaching as a Subversive Activity* (1969). I recommend it to you, even if you are not interested in the study of education, because it remains an excellent guide to what the authors refer to as *crap-detecting*, that is, the ability to detect *bullshit*. And that ability, I would add, is very much a part of subversive thinking. And I should add that this brand of subversive thinking draws on two other major thinkers. One is Alfred Korzybski (1933/2023), founder of general semantics, whose magnum opus published in 1933 is *Science and Sanity*. The other is someone I have already mentioned, Marshall McLuhan whose most important work was published in 1964, *Understanding Media: The Extensions of Man*. And the term "understanding" is very much to the point, because the "sub" in "subversive" corresponds to the "under" in "understanding," so both words indicate a need to get to the bottom of things. The root meaning of "verse" in "subversive" refers to the idea of turning, which may seem at odds with the idea of "standing" in "understanding". But we have to be able to stand before we can turn, and we have to know where we stand, before we know how to turn.

To this, I would add the quote from the philosopher Hannah Arendt (1978): "There are no dangerous thoughts; thinking itself is dangerous" (p. 176). I suppose you could take this to mean that thinking itself is subversive, and it certainly is in a world where so many go about their lives in a thoughtless manner. But in stressing the act of thinking over any particular thought anyone might have, Arendt was in effect echoing McLuhan's famous maxim, *the medium is the message*. For me, this sums up the foundation of subversive thinking, that we need to pay attention to the question of *how*, that the way that we do things has much to do with what we actually end up doing. And the way that we do things has much to do with what we end up with, when we do the things that we do. Moreover, the way that we do things has much to do with who we are, and who we become. *The medium is the message* reminds us of the fact that there are hidden structures or relationships that underlie whatever it is we are focusing on, that there are routines that have long ago faded into the background, becoming invisible environments that we inhabit.

The idea that the medium is the message is central to the field of media ecology, which is the study of the invisible environments that we have made for ourselves. In this way, we can understand that the defining characteristic of our species is the capacity for speech, that it is language and symbolic communication that makes us human. And that the development of systems of notation and the written word accompanied the shift from tribal, nomadic, hunter-gatherer societies to the first settlements, farms, and cities, what we have traditionally called civilization. And that the invention of the printing press was the agent of change that resulted in the transformation from the medieval world to the modern one. And that the electronic media have brought an end to the modern world, beginning a new era in human history, and resulting in a series of ongoing cultural mutations as the electronic media environment continues to evolve.

The effects are felt on a smaller, more personal level as well. Studies of brain structure and function have borne out McLuhan's intuitions, that different media can actually rewire the brain in different ways, as well as alter the way that we use our senses (Small & Vorgan, 2008; Wolf, 2007). So, for example, learning to read trains our eyes to focus on a fixed point, a form of vision that does not come naturally to us. One of the results of the fixed point of view is the development of perspective in art, which only occurred following the rebirth of book learning that we call the Renaissance (McLuhan, 1962, 1964). Not only do we use different parts of our brain when we become literate, but there also are differences in the parts of the brain used to read the alphabet and to read Chinese logographic writing, where each character stands for an entire word, and there are added iconic meanings, as opposed to the alphabet which is almost entirely phonetic. There even is a difference in brain function and memory between reading a text on paper and reading the same text on an e-reader (Small & Vorgan, 2008; Wolf, 2007).

What it all boils down to is that our forms of communication are not just means by which we express ourselves and interact with others. They are our tools for thought. Thinking, for the most part, and for most of us, is an inner monologue, or dialogue. It is just talking to ourselves, silently (we hope). And it follows that we think differently in different languages (Boroditsky, 2011; Lee, 1959; Sapir, 1921; Whorf, 1956), which is why to be fluent in a language you cannot just substitute one word for another, you have to think in that language. Spoken language gives us our most basic tools for thought, writing gives us another set of tools, and so do all of our media. This understanding was central for Douglas Engelbart and Alan Kay, the pioneers who developed the GUI, the graphical user interface that the Macintosh and Windows operating systems are based on (Bardini, 2000). Their intent was to develop a computer interface that would make it an effective medium of communication, rather than just a number cruncher.

Subversive Methods

Thinking subversively, then, means using as many different tools of thought as we are able to, and using the right tools for the right job. Learning different languages is one way to diversify our cerebral portfolios, an admittedly difficult task for us Americans. McLuhan (1964) argued that studying art is essential in developing new modes of perception. Many say that conversation is a lost art (e.g., Turkle, 2015), and dialogue was the foundation of philosophy and logical analysis for Socrates and Plato. It is often said that the only thing contemporary Americans fear more than death is public speaking, and oratory represents another potential tool for our tool kit, and the same is true for poetry. With anything we need to know just a Google search away, it may seem as if there's no need for memorization, but as Walter Ong (1982) reminds us, "you know what you can recall" (p. 33). That's why Nicholas Carr (2010) argues that Google is making us stupid. There is no knowledge without a knower, and the simple rule when it comes to memory is, use it or lose it. Learning things *by heart* is a wonderful metaphor, pointing to the fact that memory involves the whole body, going beyond just mental operations. Reciting poems, singing songs, listening and playing music, all provide new ways of looking at the world. Reading out loud is an important complement to reading silently, and reading and writing in all modes represents the most powerful method of training the mind that we have ever developed. And then there is deep reading, sustained focused reading. Not the kind of reading we engage in when surfing the web or checking out X-Twitter feeds and the Facebook stream. But rather the kind of reading that comes with reading books. On paper. I know this makes me sound like an old fogey, but the fact of the matter is that we devote a great deal of time to gazing at screens. And it may help to consider the fact that all of the individuals who developed the technologies behind our new media, social media, and mobile media were readers who read physical books. A lot of them.

To think subversively, we need to employ many different tools of thought, and especially to utilize those tools of thought that others have discarded or forgotten about, as well as those tools that others have not yet discovered.

We use our tools for thought to gather information about our environment and construct a sense of what our world is like, a process that Korzybski (1933/2023) called abstracting. And what we abstract out of our environment is only a small portion of what is really out there, with different tools allowing us to abstract different types of information. Korzybski used the analogy of the map and the territory, noting that we can never fully understand the territory, that all we can do is create maps that may be better or worse at guiding us through the territory. And Korzybski especially wanted us to be conscious of the fact that *the map is not the territory*. That should seem obvious enough, but all too often we forget that there are always many different ways to map out the same territory, and that our descriptions, our words and symbols, are not the things they represent.

Tim O'Reilly (2017), one of the pioneers of new media, and the founder of O'Reilly Media, credits Korzybski with helping him to redefine the idea of free software. Back in the 90s, we used the terms freeware and shareware for that sort of thing, which usually consisted of small programs that you could download from America Online, software made by amateurs that often turned out to be cheap stuff, of low quality or limited utility. O'Reilly decided that this was not the right map for a territory that also included software like the Linux operating system, and so he came up with the phrase *open source* as a different and more positive way to map the same territory. One of his employees also coined the phrase *Web 2.0* to highlight the fact that the World-Wide Web was evolving away from static websites to more dynamic and participatory formats such as blogs, podcasts, and social networking. Now this may sound a lot like rebranding, and in a sense it is. When conservatives wanted to find a way to oppose inheritance taxes, they came up with the phrase *death tax* which struck a chord with many. For persuaders and propagandists, whether they are working for political or commercial interests, the goal is to get people to accept one particular map as the only map for the territory. But for those of us looking to foster subversive thinking, not to mention crap detecting, the goal is to remind everyone that there are many ways to map out the same territory, and that more than one road can take us to our destination, while some roads lead to nowhere at all.

We also need to recall that some of our maps do not correspond to any territory at all, at least not in a concrete sense. As we engage in abstracting, we move from the act of perception to the act of naming, and from individual names to increasing more general categories (Korzybski, 1933/2023; Johnson, 1946). And as we get more and more abstract, the actual territory becomes harder and harder to define in concrete terms. What do we mean by *freedom*? By *democracy*? By the *economy*? What is a *nation*? A *people*? What do we mean by *success*? By *love*? By *intelligence*? These abstract terms are often talked about, but there is little that can be done about them unless they are given very specific, concrete definitions. And yet we tend to act as if they represent real things in the same sense that words like *tree*, *rock*, *chair*, and *table*, may represent real things in the world. (Such problems associated with abstracting can be mitigated via operationalism, the use of operational definitions, as Wendell Johnson, 1946, and Neil Postman, 1976, explain).

Korzybski (1933/2023) also warned against the problems inherent in the simple verb, *to be*, because we tend to treat the word *is* as if it means *equals*. So, for example, if I say that Michelle *is* a woman, we tend to think that it means that Michelle *equals* woman, implying that everything you need to know about Michelle is summed up in the category of woman, a category that would also include Hillary Clinton, Meryl Streep, Rosa Parks, Sarah Palin, and Lady Gaga. And of course it is a category that excludes nearly half of the human population, including many who might have more than a little in common with her. Along the same lines, if I said that Michelle is a singer, that statement would imply that everything there is to say about singers applies to Michelle, and that there is nothing else significant about her.

Our language suggests that there are identity relationships, and that is all well and fine when dealing with abstractions such as numbers, so we can say that one plus one equals two. But out in the world, no two things are ever exactly alike. One chair or seat may more or less resemble another in this room, but there are differences that make each one unique, certainly on the subatomic level, but also minor differences that can be observed by the naked eye, and maybe not so minor if one of those differences causes the chair or seat to collapse. There are no identity relationships in nature, and our language misleads us as well simply by the fact that in giving things a name, we imply that they are static entities, rather than dynamic phenomena. Michelle today is not the same person that she was ten years ago, not the same person she was a year ago, not exactly the same person she was even yesterday. She is constantly changing and evolving, but because her name does not change and evolve with her, our language implies that *who* she is today is identical to the *who* she was in the past. There is continuity of course, but it is also true that we are constantly changing physically, biologically, but also cognitively and emotionally.

Language is a mapmaking tool that provides us with a limited and distorted view of the world, and we need to be aware of this in order to think subversively. And this is all the more the case when dealing with different languages. Back in the sixties, an ad company created a TV commercial for a woman's underarm deodorant that featured a cartoon character, a female octopus extolling the virtues of the product while spraying the deodorant under all eight of her tentacles. Since the product was going to be marketed in Japan, the company decided to use the same ad, substituting a Japanese voiceover, and they proceeded to test it on a Japanese audience. Soon after the commercial began, the audience broke out laughing, hysterically. The American advertisers were puzzled, until finally someone in the audience explained to them: "In English you call the tentacles *arms*. In Japanese we call them *legs*."

When they first started selling canned goods in some African nations, where the shoppers couldn't read the English language labels, they understood that the can with a picture of peas on the label had peas inside, the can with a picture of corn on the label had corn inside, and so on. I think you can imagine their response when they first saw a brand whose trademark was a drawing of a young child. And maybe you heard about how poorly Chevrolet fared when they introduced the Chevy Nova south of the border? Because in Spanish, *no vas* means *don't go*. These are all classic examples of the fact that we mistake the label, the name, or the map, for the territory.

Beyond the words that we use, it is our metaphors that shape the way that we view the world, especially those metaphors that we do not even realize are metaphors (Gozzi, 1999; Lakoff & Johnson, 1980). For example, consider the way that we talk about time without thinking much about it. We say that we can spend time, save time, lend time, spare time, borrow time, invest time, budget time, and spend your time profitably, not to mention ask if it is worth your while or how much time it will cost you. More generally, you can give time, take time, waste time, use time, lose time, put aside time, run out of time, have time, have enough time, have time left, etc. The underlying metaphor is that *time is money*, which means that time is a valuable resource and a limited commodity, and more generally, that time is a thing rather than a process. This metaphor did not exist before the invention of the mechanical clock in 13th century Europe, and it is, in many ways, a tragic view of time as an enemy to be resisted and fought, and conquered or be conquered by (Mumford, 1934). Contrast it with the sense that time is on my side, that it will happen in time, in its own good time, that all things must pass, and that *to everything there is a season and a time to every purpose under heaven*. These are different ways of understanding and experiencing time. But in contemporary technological societies we tend to use the *time is money* metaphor, which makes us nervous, frantic, stressed, and its power over us has much to do with the fact that we do not even think of it as a metaphor, we think of it as what time really *is*. But for any metaphor we may be using, there can always be alternatives, if we take the trouble to look for them.

After the introduction of the alphabet in ancient Greece, a whole slew of visual metaphors suddenly appeared, metaphors that are still with us to this day (Ong, 1982). And so we talk about, from my *point of view*, from my *perspective*, from where I *stand*, the way that I *see* things, the way that I *see* myself, my *self-image*, upon *reflection*, the *focus* of my argument, my *line* of reasoning, my *train* of thought, and so on. And then there are phrases such as, in the *first place*, in the *second place*, etc.—and, where exactly are those places anyway? The metaphor is so deeply embedded that we find it in the root meaning of the word *topic*, which refers to *place*, as in *topography, topology*, and *topiary*. The metaphor is derived from the visual organization of information that was made possible by the written word (Strate, 2011b). By way of contrast, instead of these visual metaphors for thought processes, we sometimes say that we *grasp* a idea, that we are in *touch* with our feelings, both tactile metaphors, and we occasionally use acoustic metaphors such as when we speak of *harmony*, that something *resonates*, and that something else creates *dissonance*.

If we recognize metaphors for what they are, we can ask, to what extent do they work? What do they overlook or obscure? And what alternatives might there be? (For more on metaphor analysis, see

Gozzi, 1999). We can also think about the metaphors we adopt when we play a role. When you enter into a new situation, a new relationship, do you play the role of a good soldier, a drill sergeant, a parent, a child, a lawyer, a coach, a teammate, a teacher, a student? The roles that we are familiar and comfortable with can become the metaphors for other roles that are new to us.

Postman (1976, 1995; Postman & Weingartner, 1969) stressed the importance of metaphors, and also of the questions that we ask. The old saying, *ask a silly question, get a silly answer*, can be generalized to indicate that the kinds of questions we ask have much to do with the kinds of answers that we get. And that is another way of saying that the medium is the message. There are many kinds of questions, and not every question is a good question. Certainly, there are loaded questions, for example asking a politician, *when are you going to stop cheating the American people?* There are of course rhetorical questions, like, *so you want to change the world?* There are yes or no questions, *are you against abortion, are you in favor of military intervention, are you opposed to marriage equality, are you now or have you ever been a member of the Communist Party?* Such questions imply that we live in a black-and-white, either-or world of two-valued orientations, which is fine for computers running on binary code, but not for human relationships or for the natural world. You do not have to be into erotic romance novels to know that there are fifty shades of grey, at the very least. Yes or no questions have their place, there are times when we want to know whether we need to turn left or right to get to our destination. But we also need to recognize the difference between different types of questions, and the value of open-ended questions, the questions that ask, *what do you think*, and *how do you feel?* Put another way, if you ask the question *how much?*, or *how many?*, you'll never get the answer to the question of *who?* Or *why?*

The importance of asking the right question is illustrated by an old joke, used in many different religions, in which a man asks a member of the clergy whether it is ok to smoke while praying, to which the response is, *no, of course not, that would be disrespectful*. And then the man asks another member of the clergy whether it is ok to pray while smoking, to which the response is, *yes, of course, prayer is always welcome, no matter what you are doing*. And Postman (1976) was fond of the no doubt apocryphal story of the European village set in a time before modern medicine took hold. The villagers there came to realize that they might be mistaken about whether someone is alive or not, and could possibly bury someone who is not dead yet. Having asked the question, *how do we make sure the people we are burying are really dead*, the answer clearly presented itself: They attached a large stake to the lid of the coffin, so that when the coffin was closed, the stake would impale the body in a way that no one could survive. Holding aside any talk of vampires, it becomes painfully apparent that asking the wrong question can be a matter of life and death. And after all, our answers come and go, changing with new discoveries and the accumulation of knowledge. But good questions are eternal, questions such as Douglas Adams' big question from his *Hitchhiker's Guide to the Galaxy*, the question of *life, the universe, and everything*.

The Three Es

As for my own hitchhiker's guide to subversive thinking, I want to emphasize what you might call the three Es, three important ideas that happen to begin with the same letter as *Electronic*, the type of media and technology that have shaped our contemporary culture, society, and mindset.

The first E is *Experience*. Our tools for thought give us different ways of experiencing the world, and as I mentioned, this informed the way that Douglas Engelbart and Alan Kay designed the graphical user interface and the mouse. For them, innovation was not about making gadgets to play with, or appliances to get a job done, it was about creating an empowering and enlightening experience (Bolter & Gromala, 2003). Steve Jobs learned this lesson well, and in many ways the great success story of Apple comes down to his dedication to the idea that their products should provide users with a compelling experience.

Among other things, the lesson they all learned from McLuhan (1962, 1964) was to pay special attention to our different senses, and the way that they differ, including the idea that there is something about electronic media that appeals to the sense of touch. We can see that in the mouse, which is an extension of the finger, in the original iPod click wheel, and in the touch screen of the iPhone and the iPad. Another important insight from McLuhan has to do with the difference between the experience of the acoustic and the visual. When we listen, we are situated at the center of our world, with sounds all around us. In this sense, all sound is surround-sound. Always being at the center, no matter where we are or where we go, we are always thrust into the midst of things, and very much a part of the world that we inhabit. This means that we need to live in harmony with the world. It is an ecological position, as well as one that is subjective, that emphasizes our own inherent subjectivity, our humanity, and the comedy of survival.

By way of contrast, when we use our eyes, not only can we open and close them, not only are we forced to choose a particular direction to look in, but vision also gives us the impression of being an outsider looking in, a spectator, a peeping tom, a voyeur. We have the illusion of standing outside of the world, apart from the world, and in opposition to the world. It is an objective position, the position required for modern science, and it means that we look at the world as made up of objects that we can act upon, take possession of, control and manipulate. Vision goes hand in hand with tragedy, the isolated individual doomed by hubris. Vision can also give us the illusion of a world that is static and unchanging, frozen in time. Sound never can, for as Walter Ong (1982) puts it, "sound only exists as it is going out of existence" (p. 32). And as he explains, when I say the word *existence*, by the time I get to *tence*, *exist* is gone for good. Sound is dynamic. Hit the pause button on a recording, and the video turns into a freeze frame, but the soundtrack is replaced with silence.

Before literacy, acoustic space was the dominant mode of experience. After literacy, visual space began to take hold, for example through Euclidean geometry, and especially after the invention of printing, which made possible Newtonian physics. Western culture has been characterized by a high degree of visualism, but one that has been countered, somewhat, by the acoustic and nonlinear qualities of electronic media. We still have a strong attachment to the visual, but many of the big breakthroughs in electronic media start with the acoustic. For example, the idea of virtual reality, having been a big buzz word back in the early nineties, has become popular again in recent years, due to devices such as Oculus Rift and the idea of the metaverse. But what everyone ignores is that the first virtual reality system was an acoustic one, and it was introduced back in the sixties. It was called *stereo*, and the idea was that by having two channels of sound coming through two speakers, it reproduced the reality of listening to a live performance through our two ears.

We have a long history of visualism, which is why we still use all of those visual metaphors I mentioned earlier. We say that seeing is believing, but people once believed that hearing is believing. Back in ancient Greece, the poet Homer was said to be blind, and that meant that he was better able to listen to the muses as they related to him the true history of the Trojan War. And the Roman goddess of Justice was depicted as blind, not only to indicate objectivity, but to represent the paramount importance of hearing the truth via spoken testimony, which to this day carries greater weight than a written confession in the courtroom. Even when it comes to the written word, in antiquity and the middle ages most literates only knew how to read out loud. It was not until the print era that silent reading became commonplace. And as a product of print culture, modern science could only deal with phenomena if they could be translated into visual form. Even sound had to be represented as waveforms, and of course via musical notation. The point is that we still need to make an extra effort to think in acoustic terms rather than in visual terms, and for that reason, the acoustic experience can be an aid to thinking subversively. But we need to understand how each one of our senses work, how they differ one from the other, and also how they can work together.

This brings me to the second E, which is *Environment*. Our experience of the world is our environment, which is to say that we can only experience our maps, not the actual territory, so we better make sure our maps are good ones, maps that can serve us well to get wherever it is that we want to go.

When we talk about communication, we often talk about it as a form of transportation or a pipeline, a way of sending messages back and forth, and this is a very limited and misleading map, and metaphor. After all, we *enter into* a conversation, a dialogue, a negotiation. And we are *in* a relationship. Any situation or context constitutes an environment that we inhabit, one that shapes the way that we interact with each other, that determines the meaning of our messages, and otherwise influences us as individuals and in groups. In the same way, when we write, we may write *in* English, *in* French, *in* Hebrew, *in* Mandarin. We are *immersed* in our languages, and when we sit down to read, we can get lost *in* a good book. We also lose ourselves *in* screens, and McLuhan particularly pointed to television as an implosive medium that sucks us into its world. And of course it becomes quite commonplace to refer to new media as environments, as we go *surfing* the internet and *exploring* cyberspace, browsing through *websites*, entering URLs on the *address* bar, *navigating* through the information *architecture*. Even something as prosaic as Microsoft Word is referred to as a word processing *environment*.

Alfred Korzybski (1933/2023) discussed our "neuro-semantic and neuro-linguistic *environments as environment*" (p. lxiv) and general semantics as taking an "organism-as-a-whole-in-an-environment" perspective (p. liv), while Wendell Johnson (1946) and Neil Postman (1976) referred to our semantic environments. We live simultaneously in biophysical environments, technological environments, and symbolic environments, all of which can be considered forms or aspects of our media environments (Strate, 2017b). Moreover, media ecology is defined as *the study of media as environments* (Postman, 1968, 1970), which really means the study of human environments, because as human beings we are constantly shaping and reshaping the world we live in, which in turn feeds back into us, changing us for better and for worse. To give one example, as writing introduced the idea of the straight line, we began to reshape our world in that image, in the image of the line of text and the right angle of the page (Carpenter, 1973; Lee, 1959; McLuhan, 1962, 1964; Schmandt-Besserat, 1996). You can see it in the proscenium arch that frames theatrical performance, which was first introduced in the literate culture of ancient Greece, in the frames that surround our paintings, in our photographs and movies, and in every screen that you might choose to look at. You can see it in our architecture, our arrangement of space, our furniture, etc., everywhere you look, you see straight lines and right angles, something you almost never find in nature. Look to tribal peoples, nonliterate, oral cultures, and you see round dwellings, the best known examples being the igloo, the teepee, the hut, or other kinds of irregular shapes and constructions. But we have followed the line in the material world, and in the line of logical reasoning that proceeds from point A to point B to point C, in the step by step process of the formula and algorithm, in the straightening out of plot lines to proceed from beginning to middle to end, in the construction of machines, which follow a step by step process, their extreme manifestation being the assembly line, and it is also reflected in the vanishing art of the chorus line. Linearity goes hand in hand with visualism, and only recently have we started to move away from it, towards the nonlinearity of the electric circuit, the feedback loop, the hypertext, the interactive and the participatory. Nonlinearity is the key to understanding our new electronic environment, and we see it in art, architecture, in literature, and in science. I do want to stress, however, that it would be a mistake to abandon linearity altogether, as it has been a powerful tool for thinking and shaping our world. In an environment dominated by linearity, nonlinearity is the tool we need to think subversively. But the more that our culture goes over to a nonlinear mode of being, the more that we need linearity as a tool to counter it. In other words, we need them both.

In talking about human environments, I assume there is no need for me to address the basic concerns regarding climate change and sustainability. The fundamental value for any form of ecology, including media ecology, is balance, and the struggle is to find balance in our own lives, to find balance locally and to find balance globally.

One of the keys to finding balance brings us the third E, which is *Event*. Environment is a spatial metaphor, and spatial metaphors tend to make us overlook the dimension of time. Time is more mysterious to us than space, harder to get a handle on, harder to think about, which is why we tend to conceptualize it as a form of space. Typically, we use the metaphor of the line, and represent events as a timeline, which oversimplifies the complexity of historical interactions. Consider even the common way of thinking about time as moving forward into the future, the past behind us. McLuhan pointed out that this made no sense, which is why he used the metaphor of the rearview mirror (McLuhan & Fiore, 1967), by which he meant that, if anything, we move backwards into the future. The past is clearly visible to us, we know where we have been, while the future is hidden from us, we cannot see what is to come. But even with the metaphor of the rearview mirror or of walking backwards, we still tend to think of time in one dimension, while we conceive of space in the three dimensions of length, width, and height. Why not think of time as multidimensional as well? Even Einstein talked about time as a dimension of space, subordinating it within the unified concept of *spacetime*. But why not *timespace* instead (Strate, 2011a, 2011b)? Back when cyberspace was a buzzword, it was commonly stated that our sense of space when interacting with new media is an illusion, one that we can share with others online (Strate, 1999). The space may not be real, but the time we spend interacting with the technology and with others through the technology is entirely real. Time is the true invisible environment.

Western languages tend to use nouns to represent the world, even when referring to phenomena that are events, such as lightning. The linguistic anthropologist Benjamin Lee Whorf (1956) studied the native American languages of the Hopi and Navajo, and discovered that they rely on verbs much more than nouns, and he pointed out that that was consistent with our contemporary understanding of the physical universe. While it may be a less accurate map in some ways to use a noun like *lightning* and thereby view the phenomenon as a thing and not an event, it is because of that erroneous map that we get someone like Benjamin Franklin going out into a thunderstorm to try to capture lightning in a bottle. And in doing so, he started us down the road that led us to electric technology and the electronic media. Thinking of the world in nouns rather than verbs is powerful, but one way to think subversively is to try to think in verbs instead, because verbs are intimately related to the concept of time, to the view of the world as composed of actions and events rather than objects and things.

And what is time, but another word for change? If there is no change—which is what scientists imagine was the case before the big bang, and will be the case when the universe eventually comes to an end—if there is no change, there is no time. If change comes to an end, time stops. Our environment is an event that is happening, not a static thing, and the same is true of all that we create. A message that we send, a book that we write, a blog post, a status update, a building or monument, everything is, ultimately, an action or an event. And like all phenomena in the universe, we ourselves are all events in spacetime, or rather events in timespace, dynamic processes unfolding and evolving.

And this brings me to the end of my hitchhiker's guide to subversive thinking. It has been something of a whirlwind tour through some ideas that I consider to be very important and very useful. And I hope you find what I have had to say helpful in some way, as you set about making things better by changing your world, by changing our world, and most importantly, by healing the world.

The **And**

And ... within the discipline of general semantics, Alfred Korzybski (1933/2023) introduced the concept of *extensional devices*, modest techniques that can be used to remedy some of the problems generated by our use of language and other forms of symbolic communication. My aim in this essay is to suggest a new device that can be added to their number, and to provide a rationale for its adoption. Before doing so, it would make sense to review the ones that already are a part of our non-aristotelian system.

The first extensional device that Korzybski discussed is referred to as *indexing*, which takes written form as a subscript attached to a word. For example, we can distinguish between $thing_1$ and $thing_2$, understanding that all things *not* being equal, we should be cautious when exercising our ability to generalize and categorize. This can serve to remind us of the principle of non-identity, of the unique quality of all things, that all phenomena are one-of-a-kind events in spacetime. We can say, for example, that $chair_1$ is not $chair_2$ and use this device to help us distinguish between two different specific chairs, e.g., *this* chair and *that* chair, keeping in mind that even in the case of seemingly identical items, say two mass produced desk chairs, there will always be at least minute differences between each individual product. We can also use $chair_1$ and $chair_2$ to differentiate between two different types of chairs, e.g., $chair_1$ to refer to an overstuffed lounge chair, while $chair_2$ represents a simple folding chair. Indexing can also serve to remind us that a word can function on different levels of abstracting or logical typing, so that, for example, $chair_1$ may refer to a particular individual chair, as when we say, bring me *the* chair, while chair$_2$ may instead refer to the general category of chairs, as when we say, bring me *a* chair, meaning *any* chair. Additionally, given that words can have more than one meaning, indexing can help us to differentiate between the two, so that, for example, chair$_1$ may refer to a piece of furniture, while chair$_2$ represents the head of a committee; in this way, we can avoid confusion in a sentence like, *the chair sat on a chair*, by instead rendering it as, *the chair$_2$ sat on a chair$_1$*.

The second extensional device introduced by Korzbyski is similar to indexing, but more specific, as it distinguishes between different points in time. Hence, it is referred to as *dating*, and is used as a written superscript. So, for example, we can say that Joe Biden^{1974} is not Joe Biden^{2024}, Joe Biden^{2024} being older and presumably wiser than Joe Biden^{1974}, and more importantly to emphasize the fact that his positions on various issues may have changed, along with his occupation and his life circumstances. We implicitly understand that US\$100^{1974} is not US\$100^{2024}, which is why various statistics about costs, earnings, and profits need to be adjusted for inflation. And given the volatility of markets and currencies, we might also find that US\$100^{9AMESTFebruary29,2024} is not US\$100^{5PMESTFebruary29,2024}. This device serves to remind us that everything is a process, everything is in flux, that everything is always changing, from the subatomic particles whizzing around to the fact that planets, solar systems, and galaxies are all traveling at enormous speeds. Dating is a reminder that all phenomena are dynamic events in spacetime. It is worth noting that some scholarly style guides follow a similar format for reference citations, such as the one set up by the American Psychological Association (which I am using for this volume); for example, an in-text citation of the last book I published with the Institute of General Semantics, *Concerning Communication*, would appear as (Strate, 2022), while an earlier collection published by the IGS, *On the Binding Biases of Time*, would appear as (Strate, 2011). Although such citations are only intended to take the place of bulky footnotes and endnotes, dating as a device helps to identify the temporal context of publications, and reinforces our awareness that an individual's thought can change and grow over time, as mine most certainly has. It can also remind us that individuals are capable of changing their minds, as was the case for Neil Postman when he coauthored *Teaching as a Subversive Activity* (Postman & Weinartner, 1969), as opposed to Neil Postman when he was the author of *Teaching as a Conserving Activity* (Postman, 1979)—Neil Postman[1969] is not Neil Postman[1979].

The third major extensional device is the use of *etc.* at the end of any given sentence. This can be rendered as *et cetera*, fully written out, or more typically in its abbreviated form of *etc.*, and sometimes in its even more abbreviated form of *&c* (which I have used as part of the title of this book, based on the pun that it can be read as representing *and c* rather than as *et cetera*). The literal translation of the Latin phrase *et cetera* is, quite simply, *and the rest*. This device serves to remind us that all of our statements are necessarily incomplete, that whatever you say about any given subject, there is always more to be said, that words can never say all there is to say, or convey all there is to know, about any phenomenon. There are, of course, other ways to indicate the non-allness of our statements and the incompleteness of our representations of reality, for example by saying, *and so on and so forth*, or more recently by the slang expression, *yada, yada, yada*, both phrases appearing at the end of a statement. The same meaning can also be conveyed in writing nonverbally, via the ellipsis, the punction mark consisting of three consecutive periods ... The importance of what e.e. cummings referred to as "my sweet old etcetera" is underscored by the fact that the general semantics journal founded by S.I. Hayakawa, at one time edited by Neil Postman, and presently edited by Thom Gencarelli, took its name from this extensional device, e.g., *ETC: A Review of General Semantics*.

Indexing, dating, and etc. are extensional devices that Korzybski referred to as working devices, in contrast to other extensional devices referred to as safety devices. These include the use of *quotation marks* to indicate that certain terms are problematic, often because they are not clearly defined or subject to contested definitions. Quotation marks can be used for high level abstractions such as "intelligence" or "democracy" for example, and in speech can be indicated by the use of "air quotes" as a nonverbal gesture. A second safety device is *hyphenation*, used to counter the elementalistic tendencies of language to break apart what cannot be rendered asunder in reality, for example by referring to *mind-body* as an inseparable unity, and by referring to *rational-emotional* qualities, as the psychotherapist Albert Ellis did, influenced as he was by Korzybski. Albert Einstein's famous formulation, *space-time*, serves as exemplar of this device, also demonstrating that over time, in some instances, the hyphen can be omitted altogether (i.e., *spacetime*). In addition to Korzybski's five devices, the general semantics scholar Wendell Johnson (1946) added several more of his own. These include using *plurals* instead of singular (instead of asking, *what is the cause of war*, ask, *what are the causes of wars*); using quantifying terms (instead of saying, *it's hot out today*, say, *it is 95 degrees today*); using *actional* and *operational* terms (instead of saying *he is mean*, be specific and concrete, and refer to actual behaviors, such as, *he calls people names*, or, *he gets into fist fights*); using *conditional* and *qualifying* terms that provide context and state exceptions (e.g., *at this time, in our culture, in my opinion, the way that I see it, as far as I can recall*, etc.); and use of *underlining* or *italics* in writing and print to indicate that you are referring to a word as a *word*, rather than to what the word refers to (e.g., to distinguish between "the pen is on the table" and "*pen* can refer to a writing implement or an enclosure").

Having reviewed the introduction of extensional devices by Korzybski and the addition to their number by Johnson, I would now like to make a modest contribution of my own, one that is closely related to the working device of *etc*. Once again, when fully written out, the Latin phrase consists of two words, *et cetera*, the word *cetera* meaning *the rest*, preceded by the conjunction *et*, meaning *and*. As an extensional device, the *etc* is added to the end of a given statement or phrase, in contrast to the traditional way that we indicate that a narrative has reached its final moment or a work has come to its conclusion, i.e., through the phrase, *the end*. You might say that *the etc* replaces *the end* with *the and*, but that would be somewhat inaccurate, given the penultimate position of the Latin word *et*, preceding the word *cetera*—the *and* is not the very *end* of a phrase like *and the rest*. Indeed, it bears a certain resemblance to a similar Latin phrase, *et al.*, an abbreviation of *et alia*, meaning *and others*, a term often used for citations. While *et al* implies some form of delimitation rather than a list that extends indefinitely, and *etc* is relatively more open-ended, *etc* still suggests that there is an unnamed but not infinite range of possibilities represented by the *cetera*, by whatever constitutes *the rest*. For this reason, the extensional device I am introducing here provides a further contrast with the sense of closure, completion, and allness represented by the phrase *the end*, because what I am referring to as *the and* is meant to be positioned at the *beginning* of a sentence.

Of course, we typically are taught in school that we should never, ever start a sentence with a conjunction. You may even have learned the easy mnemonic device for keeping track of coordinating conjunctions, the acronym FANBOYS, which stands for *for, and, nor, but, or, yet*, and *so*. And if you have taken this lesson to heart, and stand ready to come down on me as the grammar police, seeking to arrest this sort of usage, please understand: There is no clear rationale for this prohibition, or for similar rules against starting a sentence with words like *whether* or *however*. It is nothing more than an aesthetic preference imposed on us, one that has been extended, by some, even so far as to disallow beginning a sentence with the word *also*. It should be patently obvious that we are quite capable of starting sentences with conjunctions in the English language, and ending them with prepositions, for that matter. And there is nothing wrong with doing so. As I have discussed elsewhere, rules such as these were imposed by prescriptive grammarians several centuries ago in a misguided attempt to try to make English follow the same syntax as Latin (see Strate, 2022).

For my part, I do not particularly recall learning the rule that you are not supposed to begin a sentence with words like *and* or *but*, although I assume that it did come up in grade school at some point.

But by the time I had begun to find my voice as a writer and scholar, I had no reservations whatsoever about starting sentences that way, and especially using the word *and*. As a graduate student and young academic new to publishing, such instances would be "corrected" by copy editors before appearing in print, and I had no choice except to accept the changes. In one instance, I tried to convince a publisher to allow me my usage for a book chapter I had written for an edited collection about media and culture. The response I got was not unreasonable, that the editors of this book had a particular style that they were using, and that when I produced a book of my own, I could decide on my own style. And so I have. But that exchange also prompted me to consider the source of my affinity for sentences that start with *and*. And I realized that, as much as the prohibition against doing so was invoked with religious fervor by some, my own preference also had a religious dimension to it. In relating my own personal religious experience, I want to stress that I do so to support the argument that there is ample precedent for starting sentences with conjunctions, as well as to explain my own affinity for doing so.

In Jewish worship, the central prayer is the recitation of the *Shema*, taken from Deuteronomy 6:4, which translates as, "Hear O Israel, the Lord our God, the Lord is One". In the liturgy, it is immediately followed by a second line that does not appear in the Torah and was added in antiquity to form a call and response, which translates as, "Blessed is the name of God's glorious kingdom forever and ever". What then follows is one of our most important prayers, the *V'ahavta*, which is taken from the passage in the Torah that immediately follows the *Shema*, Deuteronomy 6:5, starting with a new sentence that in Hebrew begins with the word *v'ahavta*. But actually *v'ahavta* is two words, because the word *and* in Hebrew takes the form of a prefix represented by the letter *vav*—the *v'* in *v'ahavta* means *and*. While English translations tend to omit the initial conjunction, the poetically rendered King James version preserves this aspect of the Hebrew opening, and its continued usage in the lines that follow. Below I reproduce those lines, but use line breaks typical of poetry rather than prose to better illustrate the repeated use of *the and* in this portion:

> And thou shalt love the Lord thy God with all thine heart,
> and with all thy soul,
> and with all thy might.
> And these words, which I command thee this day, shall be in thine heart:
> And thou shalt teach them diligently unto thy children,
> and shalt talk of them when thou sittest in thine house,
> and when thou walkest by the way,
> and when thou liest down,
> and when thou risest up.
> And thou shalt bind them for a sign upon thine hand,
> and they shall be as frontlets between thine eyes.
> And thou shalt write them upon the posts of thy house,
> and on thy gates. (Deuteronomy 6:5–9)

The use of *the and* here is not unique to this passage, nor is it unusual within the original ancient Hebrew text of the *Holy Scriptures*. For example, a Jewish-language columnist who goes by the pen name of Philologos (2022) offered a comparison between the King James Version and *The Koren Tanakh* of a portion of Exodus (19:17-19), from the Torah reading named *Yitro*. Here is the translation from *The Koren Tanakh* published in 2010:

> Then Moshe led the people out of the camp to meet God, and they stood at the foot of the mountain. Mount Sinai was enveloped in smoke because the Lord had descended on it in fire. Smoke billowed up from it as if from a furnace, and the mountain shook violently as one. As the sound of the ram's horn grew louder and louder, Moshe spoke and God answered him aloud. (quoted in Philologos, 2022, para. 5)

And here now, again with my own addition of line breaks, is the King James Version:

> And Moses brought forth the people out of the camp to meet with God;
> And they stood at the nether part of the mount.
> And Mount Sinai was altogether on a smoke, because the Lord descended on it in fire:
> And the smoke thereof ascended as the smoke of a furnace,
> And the whole mount quaked greatly.
> And then the voice of the trumpet sounded long
> And waxed louder and louder, Moses spake,
> And God answered him by a voice.
> (quoted in Philologos, 2022, para. 5)

Philologos (2022) goes on to discuss the fact that the King James Version has five more instances of the *and* than the recent translation:

> A paradox? Not for anyone accustomed to traditional English Bible translations, whether the King James version or any other. All such translations have many more *ands* than does normal English prose—and they have it because the Hebrew Bible has a similar abundance of the conjunction *v'*, *va*, or *u*, all differently vocalized forms of a prefixed consonant *vav* that have traditionally been translated as "and." Indeed, among the first two questions that modern Bible translators have to ask and answer before setting to work are: 1) Should a prefixed *vav* at the beginning of a word in the Bible always be translated by "and?" and 2) If not, should it sometimes be translated at all? (para. 7)

And Philologos continues by pointing out that biblical Hebrew is "a language poor in conjunctions" (para. 10), explaining

> Although it has its own ways of expressing logical and temporal relationships between parts of sentences, something that is largely done in English by means of commas and periods, dependent clauses, and conjunctions like "when," "while," "as," "though," "despite," and so forth, biblical Hebrew rarely puts together sentences by such means. It prefers coordinate clauses joined by a *vav*—or, in more technical language, paratactic rather than hypotactic constructions in which the *vav* can do the work of various English conjunctions and mean other things beside "and." (para. 10)

Writing for a popular outlet, the columnist does not make a distinction between meaning and function here, a distinction that I believe to be important. By way of an analogy, when we say that the Hebrew word *shalom* means *hello*, *goodbye*, and *peace*, what we really mean is that the Hebrew word for *peace* performs the same *functions* as our words *hello* and *goodbye*, the phatic function of a salutation or greeting said upon meeting someone, and a valediction said at the time of departure. It follows that the Hebrew word for *and* performs multiple functions, but still conveys the same primary meaning. Philologos (2022) also notes that the use of the prefix in biblical Hebrew also serves a grammatical function when it is followed by a verb, in that it "can change its tense from past or perfect to future or imperfect, and vice versa" (para. 8). Here too this added function does not necessarily cancel out the meaning and function of the prefix as a conjunction.

While the columnist mainly is concerned with linguistic differences that are dealt with differently by different translators, these differences also relate to the contrasts between orality and literacy discussed by media ecology scholars such as Marshall McLuhan (1962) and Walter Ong (1982). The very question of whether or not we ought to begin a sentence with a particular word would be meaningless in an oral culture, and not only because the very idea of correct or incorrect grammar did not exist until well after the introduction of typography. Ong explains that in the absence of writing, which transforms ephemeral sounds into permanent visual markings, there is no clear conception of the concept of a word, let alone a sentence; rather, the unit of expression would be an utterance, which could be a single syllable or entire song or speech. And the Hebrew Bible originates in a period in which alphabetic literacy was new, and incorporates material that originated as oral tradition and dictated speech, as well as written work composed in the traditional oral style. The Torah was meant to be read out loud more or less exclusively, as reading silently was all but unknown in antiquity; in fact, it was not only read out loud, but chanted, as an aid to memory. Add to this the fact that in antiquity punctuation marks were all but unknown, and completely absent in the Torah. In their absence, and in contradistinction to the modern rule, the use of *vav* has the added function of indicating a line break or what we would consider the start of a new sentence. And while the traditional translations of the Bible that include the repetitive use of the word *and* were produced within a literate culture following the printing revolution in early modern Europe (Eisenstein, 1979), Elizabethan English had not yet been fully influenced by typographic literacy, and a powerful acoustic sensibility remained (McLuhan, 1962; Ong, 1982). The more recent translations, on the other hand, are grounded in modern English, a language that had been completely transformed by printing by the 19th century, which is why they opt for more variety, not only to better suit the contemporary English idiom and ear, but also the reader's eye.

In regard to the repetitive structure of the Hebrew bible, Ong (1982) argues that it is characteristic of the psychodynamics of oral cultures and the oral mindset, specifically noting that thought and expression in oral cultures tend to be "additive rather than subordinative" (p. 37). By way of illustration, he compares two translations of the first five lines of Genesis. The first is from a contemporary of the King James Version, the 17th century Douay version (again, I have structured the passage with poetic line breaks):

In the beginning God created heaven and earth.
And the earth was void and empty,

> And darkness was upon the face of the deep;
> And the spirit of God moved over the waters.
> And God said: Be light made.
> And light was made.
> And God saw the light that it was good;
> And he divided the light from the darkness.
> And he called the light Day,
> And the darkness Night;
> And there was evening
> And morning one day. (Ong, 1982, p. 37)

The second version was a contemporary rendering from the *New American Bible*, circa 1970:

> In the beginning, when God created the heavens and the earth, the earth was a formless wasteland, and darkness covered the abyss, while a mighty wind swept over the waters. Then God said, "Let there be light," and there was light. God saw how good the light was. God then separated the light from the darkness. God called the light "day" and the darkness he called "night". Thus evening came and morning followed—the first day. (Ong, 1982, p. 37)

Ong (1982) notes that in place of the repeated use of *and* in the Douay version, following the example of the original Hebrew text that was "produced in a culture with a still massive oral residue" (p. 37), the contemporary version "renders it 'and', 'when', 'then', 'thus', or 'while', to provide a flow of narration with the analytic, reasoned subordination that characterizes writing … and that appears more natural in twentieth-century texts" (p. 37). Ong stresses the point that complex diction incorporating a series of subordinate clauses is largely a product of writing and literacy, whereas oral composition, performance, and tradition favor redundancy and simplicity. And it is often the case that the kind of language that works best in oral cultures, for example language that utilizes clichés and formulaic expressions, is exactly the kind of language that we are instructed to avoid in literate cultures, especially cultures in which alphabetic literacy has been amplified by typography. Moreover, oral cultures being dependent entirely on collective memory for the preservation of knowledge, rely upon a multitude of mnemonic devices, many associated with poetry and song. In this instance, parallel structure and alliteration is very much typical of biblical Hebrew, the same being true for Old English (e.g., *Beowulf*), in contrast to the use of rhyme in modern English. The passages from Genesis and Deuteronomy use the repetition of *and* to form a parallel structure that appeals to the ear rather than the eye, because, as noted, the Torah was written to be read out loud to a gathering, a congregation. And what was read out loud was also meant to be remembered. The V'ahavta prayer calls for "these words" to be repeated over and over again, that they should *be in your heart*, meaning that you should know them *by heart*, because we remember with our whole bodies, not just our minds.

The English translations of the Torah and Hebrew prayers that I encountered in my youth followed the King James and Douay versions, and were altogether memorable, so much so that they came to inform my own cadence, diction, and voice as a writer. This accounts for my affinity for using conjunctions to lead off sentences. And I would suggest that we focus too much on providing variety of expression in our prose in contemporary culture, and not enough on the poetic form of language, and especially not enough on the importance of memory and recall. But returning to the topic of extensional devices, what I want to help us to remember is that our statements, our descriptions, our explanations are always incomplete. And just as we can never truly have the last word, it is also the case that we never truly have the first word. And whatever words we use are almost entirely words that we did not invent ourselves, words that have been in existence long before we were born, and will presumably continue to be used long after we are gone.

Starting sentences with a conjunction can serve to remind us that whatever we say is always in response to something that was said before, is always predicated on prior discussion, and that we are always coming into the human conversation in the middle, in the midst of things, *in medias res*. It follows that there is always a context that exists prior to every utterance, a situation that is present before any message is sent or received, a relationship that is established before communication can occur, a medium out of which messages and meanings are constructed, an environment that precedes and contains any set of agents performing acts, symbolic acts included. The environment is often invisible, not because it is transparent, but because it is taken for granted, becoming routine and fading into the background. The context is often hidden, to the extent that it becomes easy to forget that there was one prior to a given speech act. Beginning a statement with a conjunction serves to remind us of that which is absent, and this is sorely needed. Because it is the thing that is missing that is always the hardest to recognize. It is akin to the Sherlock Holmes story where the solution has to do with the fact that a dog that was present did *not* bark. As Gregory Bateson (1972, 1979) argues, in the symbolic realm, the things we do *not* do have significance, the apology you do *not* provide, the question you do *not* answer, the income tax forms that you do *not* file. These are differences that make a difference. I.A. Richards (1952) emphasized the need to provide context before communication in putting forth his version of the concept of *feedforward*.

We are always, if you forgive the cliché, standing on the shoulders of giants. And this extensional device that I am proposing therefore also serves to remind us of the fundamental foundation of general semantics, *time-binding*, the idea that all that we have and all that we are is based on the achievements of those who came before us (Korzybski, 1921, 1950, 1993/2023). And that our job is to continue to make progress, eliminating error and improving the life chances for those who will come after us. For this reason alone, I believe that *the and* is a worthy addition to our list of extensional devices. To be sure, I am not advocating its repeated use in a return to the diction of the Torah, or the King James and Douay bibles. But I am suggesting that it can be used judiciously, and that the nonsensical rule about never beginning a sentence with a conjunction should be discarded and never spoken of again. And most importantly, that we internalize *the and*. And that we remember, with humility, that whatever we have to say is not as original as we may think, and that it is always based on whatever has been said before. And that we are always coming in in the middle of a conversation. And that there always is a pre-existing context, medium, environment, of which we may not be aware. And that what we believe to be the end will always be …

The And

www.ingramcontent.com/pod-product-compliance
Lightning Source LLC
Chambersburg PA
CBHW040259170426

43193CB00020B/2943